FOR MY DAUGHTER

Michael O'Mara Books Limited

My darling daughter

I think of you a tiny babe,
your head by mine so gently laid.

I think of you against my breast,
the scent, the feel of you at rest.

I think of what your smile would do,
how my fond heart near broke in two.

I think of you, my life, my world,
your little hand in mine tight curled.

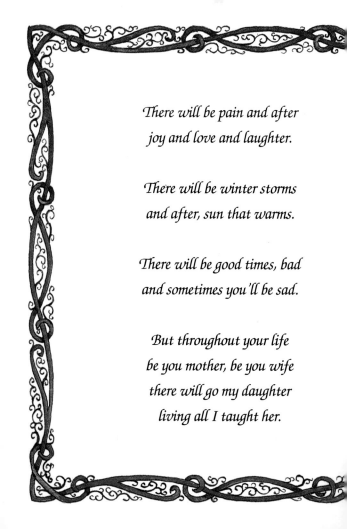

There will be pain and after
joy and love and laughter.

There will be winter storms
and after, sun that warms.

There will be good times, bad
and sometimes you'll be sad.

But throughout your life
be you mother, be you wife
there will go my daughter
living all I taught her.

So sleep, darling daughter,
let me calm your fears.

So weep, darling daughter,
I shall kiss away your tears.

So seek, darling daughter,
me always in your prayers.

So fleet, darling daughter,
are the passing years.

I remember when you were born
when I held you in my arms,
how you cried and how at morn
I rocked you, gave you balm.

I remember that first hug
skin so soft, hair so fine,
how you cradled in my arms so snug
dearest daughter, child of mine.

Shall I compare you to a perfect rose
or to the way a violet grows?

Shall I compare you to a queen of old,
to Cleopatra on her barge of gold?

Shall I compare you to the silver moon
or to the yellow sun at noon?

No, dearest daughter, I'll not dare,
you are my light beyond compare.

I loved you
  when first you were made,
  before you were ever born

I loved you
  lying in my arms, a babe
  to be kept from harm

I loved you
  when you kissed me and smiled,
  to my aching heart you brought balm

I loved you
  now as I always will
  within my circling arms.

My daughter is the apple of my eye,
jewel in my crown, the nonpareil.
My daughter is water after drought,
sunshine after rain, a brilliant
    butterfly.

I dare not tell her all that's in my
    heart,
only hold her to me, kiss and bless
    her when we part.

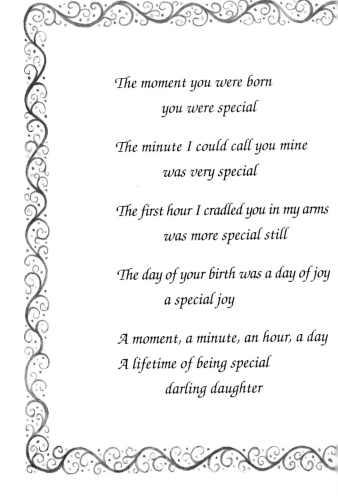

The moment you were born
you were special

The minute I could call you mine
was very special

The first hour I cradled you in my arms
was more special still

The day of your birth was a day of joy
a special joy

A moment, a minute, an hour, a day
A lifetime of being special
darling daughter

My daughter's smile lights up her eyes.

My daughter's laughter ripples like stream water.

My daughter's words are sweeter than songbirds'.

My daughter's hand stretches a world away.

My daughter's love reaches the sky above.

My daughter is my best beloved.

Dearest daughter

I watch you with such pride
    child of my dreams
I cannot my love hide
    child of my dreams
Your loveliness I treasure
    child of my dreams
My happiness without measure
    child of my dreams
Through the darkest hour gleams
    child of my dreams

*Daughter dearest, can I teach you
how not to make mistakes I made?
Will you listen if I tell you
I went through it all, your age?
Daughter dearest, may I advise you
whom to choose for friends and
whom to spurn?*

*No, daughter dearest, it is I must learn
to let you be and that way your love
earn.*

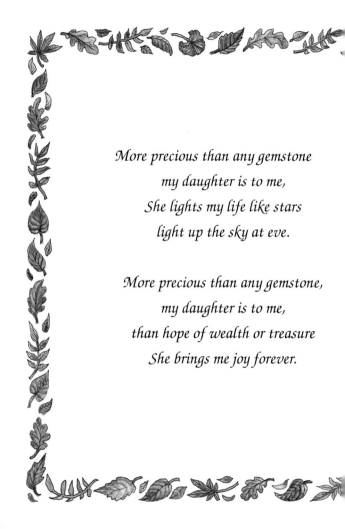

More precious than any gemstone
my daughter is to me,
She lights my life like stars
light up the sky at eve.

More precious than any gemstone,
my daughter is to me,
than hope of wealth or treasure
She brings me joy forever.

BERLITZ

INDONESIA

GW00720651

By the staff of Berlitz Guides

How to use our guide

These 192 pages cover the **highlights** of Indonesia, grouped by island. Although not exhaustive, our selection of sights will enable you to make the best of your trip.

The **sights** to see are described between pages 26 and 140. Those most highly recommended are pinpointed by the Berlitz traveller symbol.

The **Where to Go** section on page 25 will help you plan your visit according to the time available.

For **general background** see the sections Indonesia and the Indonesians (p. 8) and History (p. 14).

Entertainment and **activities** (including eating out) are recounted between pages 141 and 153.

The **practical information**, hints and tips you will need before and during your trip begin on page 154. This section is arranged alphabetically with a list for easy reference.

The **map section** at the back of the book (pp. 176–189) will help you find your way around and locate the principal sights.

Finally, if there is anything you cannot find, look in the **index** (pp. 190–192).

Printed in Switzerland by Weber S.A., Bienne.

2nd edition (1992/1993)

CONTENTS

CONTENTS

CONTENTS

Text:	Catherine McLeod
Staff Editor:	Barbara Ender
Layout:	D & N Publishing
Photography:	Ronald McLeod
Additional photos:	Berlitz cover, pp. 81, 84–85, 126, 144 TOP/R. Tixador; pp. 8, 100–101 TOP/McLeod; p. 51 TOP/Allegre; p. 94 TOP/M. Fraudeau; pp 151, 152 TOP/P. Hussenot
Cartography:	Visual Image

Acknowledgements
We would like to thank Anna Bertrand and Souphie Wahyo for their help in the preparation of this guide.

Found an error or an omission in this Berlitz guide? Or a change or new feature we should know about? Our editor would be happy to hear from you. Write to: Berlitz Publishing Company Ltd., London Road, Wheatley, Oxford OX9 1YR. Be sure to include your name and address, since in appreciation for a useful suggestion, we'd like to send you a free travel guide.

Although we have made every effort to ensure the accuracy of all the information in this book, changes occur incessantly. We cannot therefore take responsibility for facts, prices, addresses and circumstances in general that are constantly subject to alteration.

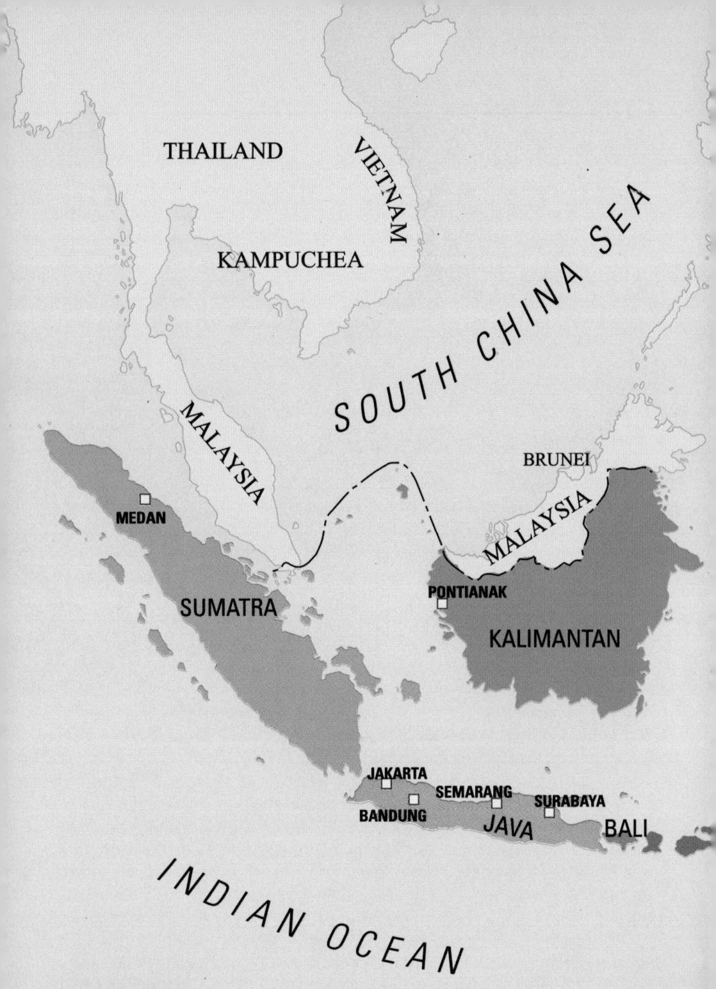

THAILAND

VIETNAM

KAMPUCHEA

SOUTH CHINA SEA

MALAYSIA

BRUNEI

MEDAN

MALAYSIA

SUMATRA

PONTIANAK

KALIMANTAN

JAKARTA

SEMARANG

SURABAYA

BANDUNG

JAVA

BALI

INDIAN OCEAN

INDONESIA

6

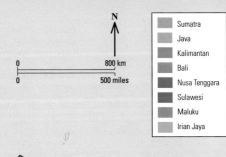

PHILIPPINES

PACIFIC OCEAN

MALUKU

SULAWESI

NUSA TENGGARA

IRIAN JAYA

PAPUA
NEW
GUINEA

AUSTRALIA

	Sumatra
	Java
	Kalimantan
	Bali
	Nusa Tenggara
	Sulawesi
	Maluku
	Irian Jaya

N

0   800 km
0   500 miles

7

INDONESIA AND THE INDONESIANS

Indonesia is like a great jigsaw puzzle spilled out of the box, its pieces scattered over some 5,000 km (3,200 miles) of equatorial ocean between Malaysia and Australia. It's the world's biggest archipelago republic, officially made up of 13,677 islands—although recent satellite pictures disclose more. Some are so large they are mini-continents, but the vast majority are mere specks with no official names and no inhabitants. The Indonesians call their country *tanah air kitah*, "our land and water", and include intervening stretches of sea when they calculate its area, about 8 million sq km (3 million sq miles), of which a quarter is land mass. It takes time to grasp its

geographic layout, especially since the names of several of the islands changed after Independence in 1950.

Sweeping from west to east, Sumatra, Java, Bali, then the Nusa Tenggara mini-archipelago (made up of Lombok, Sumbawa, Komodo, Sumba, Flores and Timor) form a chain reaching towards Irian Jaya, the western half of New Guinea. The chain encloses Kalimantan, which takes up three-quarters of the island of Borneo, Sulawesi (formerly the Celebes), and Maluku (the Moluccas).

Indonesia is the fifth most heavily populated country in the world with 195 million people, though the density varies tremendously from one island to another. The majority

Land of the unexpected, of temples, markets, and old, overlapping civilizations.

is concentrated on Java, Bali and Madura. A governmental transmigration policy resettles people on the less populated islands, and Indonesians have been alerted to the importance of only two children to a family to control the birth explosion.

Superimposed on the United States or on Europe, Indonesia would stretch roughly from San Francisco to New York or from Madrid to Moscow. Imagine the prodigious diversity of landscape, vegetation and animal life involved, and you begin to understand the complexity of Indonesia. Complicated crosscurrents of history and religion add to what can at first seem a bewildering encounter.

Bewildering but enthralling. There's sea and jungle, history and high-rise. There are stories of headhunters and demons, an abundance of national monuments and a sprinkling of Art Deco buildings from the Dutch occupation. Dark-hulled sailing ships ply between the islands like something out of a Conrad romance; motorcycles laden with whole families dare all in modern traffic jams. In Sumatra lurk tigers, orang-utans and crocodiles, Komodo is home to carnivorous dragons, on Irian Jaya birds of paradise flaunt their improbable plumage.

It's enthralling for the variety of people—the aristocrats of Yogyakarta continuing more than a thousand years of tradition; golden-skinned Balinese; Christianized Bataks from Sumatra thundering "Nearer My God to Thee" in harmonized chorus; the duckherd and the dancer; disco-goers disconcerting their elders with the latest westernized gear; the *wayang* puppeteer dramatizing age-old Hindu stories for a rapt audience. It's fascinating because of its cultural richness, and if "culture" is one of those vague words that send prickles up your spine, pin it down to precise achievements—the mighty Buddhist temple of Borobudur, the biggest ancient monument in the southern hemisphere; the faded glory of the sultans' palaces; the sweeping, saddle-backed houses of West Sumatra. Or take your personal interpretation of culture from the formal grace of a court dancer or the shimmer of gong music, as elusive as mist and starlight.

Intricately interwoven are the religions, successively layered over older beliefs of animism and ancestor worship. Indonesia is the biggest Islamic nation in the world, Muslims forming about 90 per cent of the population. Bali, however, is almost entirely Hindu, and everywhere there are Buddhists and Christians. Spirituality permeates every aspect of life. Syncretism, or the absorption of many faiths, is particularly complex in Java. But there is no state religion, freedom of thought being guaranteed by the Constitution and by the national philosophy of *Pancasila,* the Five Principles. Indonesians don't care what you believe in but would be most disturbed if you said you believed in nothing.

Tradition is alive and well and thriving in Indonesia. *Adat,* customary law, varies from one area to another, governing many everyday matters such as ceremonies for birth, marriage, death, inheritance, irrigation, diet and land ownership. It fosters superstition, for often the logical basis of the *adat* rule has been forgotten, but it also encourages solidarity within a community and gives a sense of continuity and security. Tolerance, too, is a national characteristic. You'll find the people polite, helpful, and flatteringly curious about the world you come from. Smile first, and you'll be astonished at the radiance of the beam that replies.

The country's tight-knit families and communities honour the past and, for the most part, conform with decisions on the present, while respect for one another—and for visitors—is the rule. An Indonesian may come from any one of 336 ethnic groups speaking innumerable languages and dialects as well as Bahasa Indonesia, the official, melodious language adapted from Malay. But you'll always find someone in a tourist area who understands English, which has replaced Dutch as second language.

The further you travel, the more you'll be intrigued, and the more you'll realize why Indonesia—open though it is to Western influences—is concerned with protecting its unique moral and artistic heritage. Though the country recognizes the advantages of technological achievement and is heading constructively towards the future, it strives to preserve its cultural integrity from encroachment by the "sophisticated" world, scaling technological planning to the needs of average Indonesians, 80 per cent of whom work on the land. And you'll still see poverty, notably in Jakarta.

This is the east. Enter gently into a society where modesty, calmness and correct behaviour win friends, especially on Java with its heritage of a long, ultra-refined society. Rectitude and good taste are the greatest virtues you can bring with you. Temper them with a desire to understand and admit that western ways are not applicable to all circumstances. Settle for accepting *jam karet,* literally "rubber time". Indonesians have a natural dislike of being alone—so you'll often find half-a-dozen friends and relatives pitching in on one person's job. Being together or *among-among* is a way of life.

The Asian concept of "face" exists. Indonesians tend to cover up when they don't know something and are upset if you push them too far. Sometimes a polite "yes" covers the fact that the person you're questioning doesn't like to give a straightforward "no". They also do their best to protect you from "loss of face", known in Indonesian as *malu.* Of course people expect you to be different and would be inconsolable if you weren't. Just how

11

different you are will be brought home when you visit outlying districts and find yourself the focal point of a crowd busy discussing every stitch of your clothing and every gesture you make.

Images linger long after your visit is over. Lamplit foodstalls at night; a child running home from school in spotless white from top to toe, head covered with a banana leaf to keep off the rain; the Java sea rolling pewter-coloured under a sullen sky then flashing into sheets of fire in the setting sun; a high-cheeked Tenggerese squatting immobile on the crater rim of his holy volcano; fetid canals, the well-meant legacy of the Dutch; waterfalls dashing clean and white with bright butterflies dancing in the spray.

This is Indonesia, where universal truths come alive in the flickering symbolism of the shadow puppets. In

Java, a sultan is married annually to the goddess of the South Sea; in Bali the gods are daily honoured with dance, music and offerings. Irian Jaya's snow-capped peaks glow within sight of impenetrable tropical jungle. You can't expect to come to terms with it all in a hurry, nor to see it all on one trip. Maybe you'll seek out the proboscis monkeys of East Kalimantan or the rare black orchid; glimpse a white rhino in West Java; dive into the undersea gardens of North Sulawesi. Let yourself be led to some of the lesser-known attractions—this is one of the places where you can still experience the sometimes unsettling but infinitely rewarding joy of being a bona fide traveller.

More than just a crop, rice is linked to all aspects of Balinese life: to beauty, art and religion.

HISTORY

Present-day Indonesia was one of the first homes of mankind. Remains of the so-called Java Man were found in 1891 at Trinil, Central Java. *Pithecanthropus erectus,* as this ungainly creature is known, was neither ape nor quite human. The species walked—or rather, shuffled—upright and lived some 500,000 years ago at the beginning of the glacier age when Java was still connected to the mainland. But he was no ancestor of present-day Indonesians; nor was Solo Man (named after the town of Solo), who roamed Java some 400,000 years later. That honour goes to Wajak Man, whose remains, about 10,000 years old, were discovered in East Java. He was probably also the forebear of the Australian aborigenes.

The descendants of Wajak Man were joined by two types of immigrants who came from the north, spreading into Sumatra, Borneo, Java and Celebes. The first wave, a neolithic people referred to as proto-Malays, settled inland; they are the ancestors of the Batak of Sumatra, the Dayak of Borneo and the Toraja of Sulawesi. The next wave, labelled deutero-Malays, came from a more developed Bronze Age culture; they preferred to settle along the coast.

Kingdoms by the Sea

In early times the larger islands were divided into a number of kingdoms with an economy based on rice growing (it is believed that some of the paddy fields in central Java have been cultivated for the past 2,000 years). The islands' geographical position on important trade routes brought significant contact with other civilizations. India was trading with the islands by the second century AD, and Indian immigrants intermarried with the Indonesian aristocracy; their descendants formed the governing class. For 1,400 years the Indonesians assimilated and adapted much of Indian culture, notably in the fields of law, medicine, the decorative arts, navigational techniques, methods of agriculture, philosophy, and their religion, Hinduism. Buddhism was introduced by Chinese and Indian pilgrims, and the two religions coexisted peacefully among the aristocracy, eventually syncretizing into the belief that Shiva and Buddha were incarnations of the same being. However, the popular background of animism and ancestor worship was never denied.

Many dynasties rose and fell over the centuries. The first recorded was Taruma Negara, near present-day Jakarta. One of the most powerful was the Buddhist Srivijaya Empire, which originated in Palembang on Sumatra and flourished between the 7th and 13th centuries. It is first mentioned in the writings of the

The Asmat people of Irian Jaya believe that the universe was created by a master carver.

14

Chinese Buddhist pilgrim I-ching, who visited Palembang in 671. Srivijaya established trade relations not only with the other states of the archipelago but also with China and India, where it founded monasteries. Traders passing through the Straits of Malacca were forced to pay a toll to the king. Srivijaya was finally destroyed by the Javanese in the 14th century, and the royal family and traders crossed to Malaya, where they established the port of Malacca.

Central Java was governed in the 8th and 9th centuries by the Sailendra dynasty, also Buddhists, who founded the Mataram kingdom and built the mighty temple of Borobudur. In 856, after a battle with a rival royal line who worshipped the Hindu god Shiva, the last surviving Sailendra prince fled to Sumatra, where he became the king of Srivijaya. In the 10th century, the Javanese kingdom moved to east Java, ruling first from Surabaya, then from Kediri and Singhasari, finally moving to Majapahit until 1500. This last was the greatest of the east Javanese kingdoms, possessing great agricultural wealth. It was both Hindu and Buddhist. At the fall of the Majapahit empire, many of its aristocrats fled to Bali; these refugees are the ancestors of today's Balinese élite.

Islam was introduced to Indonesia in the 13th century. First adopted by the rulers of Aceh on the northern tip of Sumatra, it spread into Java in the 14th and 15th centuries, especially along the north coast, which had most contact with traders. Eventually almost every major population group in Indonesia became Muslim, except for the Balinese who remained faithful to the Hindu culture.

The Europeans Arrive

Somewhere around 1292, Marco Polo visited Sumatra and stayed there for five months, waiting for suitable weather to continue his voyage. He reported that the island was divided into eight kingdoms, ruled by eight crowned kings, and that it abounded in treasures and costly products, including ebony and spices. The inhabitants of the city, he noted, had been converted to Islam, while the mountain dwellers lived "like beasts", worshipping the first thing they saw when they woke up in the morning and consuming human flesh. Their staples were rice and meal from the sago palm; they also drank palm wine, which, according to Polo, was a "sovereign remedy for dropsy, consumption, and the spleen".

Until the beginning of the 16th century, Indonesia was out of reach of the Europeans, who were very backward as far as navigation was concerned. In 1497, the Portuguese explorer Vasco da Gama opened up the sea route from western Europe to the East, though he never went further than Goa in India, where he founded a settlement. Thanks to their superior artillery, the Portuguese had no difficulty taking Malacca in 1511, and by the 1520s they were well established in the Spice Islands (Moluccas) and at Sunda Kelapa, now the old port area of Jakarta. An Islamic prince, Fatahillah, from the coastal area near Cirebon, forced them out in 1527, and Portuguese dominance throughout lasted less than a century. It had little cultural effect on the Indonesians, except to influence music and the language, which adopted many Portuguese words. In fact, Portuguese remained in use in business circles up to the early 19th century.

Dutch Supremacy

However short-lived, the Portuguese presence was enough for the English and Dutch to work up a competitive interest in these spice-laden islands. Holland won the race, and the United East India Company (*Vereenigde Oostindisches Compagnie* or VOC) implanted a string of "factories" or trading posts with headquarters in Batavia (now Jakarta). To be fair, Netherlands merchants braved the difficult climate and frequently fatal tropical fevers for the sake of commerce rather than colonialism. Inevitably, playing one Javanese sultan against another, they split the Javanese Mataram empire into three parts and gained power and land far beyond the VOC's limited outward ambitions, for it was a private company. Gradually it controlled all of Java with centres on other islands. By the end of the 17th century the world was referring matter-of-factly to the Indonesian archipelago as "the

Dutch East Indies". As the company acquired more land and spice prices dropped, new crops were introduced. Corruption and poor administration finally bankrupted the VOC, but by then the Dutch were well and truly established and in 1799 their government took over.

Britain had brief control of the country for a few years during the Napoleonic Wars when France occupied Holland and laid claim to all Dutch colonies. Thomas Stamford Raffles was named Lieutenant Governor and set himself vigorously to understanding the people. His *History of Java* was published in 1817. Power was handed back to the Dutch in 1816 (although the British lingered on in South Sumatra for some years), and Raffles's greater fame is associated with Singapore which he founded as a colony in 1819.

The following period of Dutch rule is divided into three periods. The so-called Cultivation System (1830–70) forced Javanese peasants to produce cash crops such as sugar, coffee and tea for delivery to the Netherlands, thereby cutting back on traditional rice-growing and subsistence agriculture and turning the whole of Java into a vast plantation for Dutch benefit. Real hardship, even starvation, was imposed on the people, but the Netherlands became rich in the process. During the Liberal period (1870–1900), Indonesia was opened to individual investment, and private plantations replaced state monopolies. The Dutch were not all heartless oppressors, nor were all the Indonesians blameless victims. High-placed Javanese were in a prime position to make use of the situation themselves and did so. And the Dutch were not unique in their colonial policies. All the great European powers built up empires with a similar urge for territorial and financial gain, an unquestioning belief in the superiority of their own culture and religion and a confused personal mixture of patronizing righteousness, on-the-spot insecurity, and fumbling goodwill.

The Ethical Period (1900–40) was marked by increasing attention to Indonesian welfare. A growing number of young people were sent to study in Holland. Then came World War II, and in 1942 the Japanese overran the islands.

Nationalism

During the whole 350 years of foreign presence, the Indonesians had never ceased thinking of independence. In 1629 the Sultan of Mataram attacked Batavia and was overcome. A rebellion in Batavia itself was quelled in 1740. In 1825, Prince Diponegoro, son of the Sultan of Yogyakarta, led a revolt which lasted five years before he was tricked into capitulation and imprisoned in Sulawesi. More intellectualized nationalist movements began with the 20th century. Among them was a study club at the celebrated Bandung Institute of Technology which, led by a young engineer, Sukarno, became the Indonesian Nationalist Party in 1927.

Holland had unwittingly laid the foundation for independence as it had introduced the Dutch language, which facilitated communication in a country possessing dozens of tongues and class traditions. Moreover, in its final, however belated and restrained burst of liberalism, Holland exposed intelligent young Indonesians to contemporary European political ideas. On the negative

This stone carving at remote Candi Sukuh bewitches visitors with its air of mystery.

side it had, again like other European powers and with mixed motives, used Christianity to its own ends, posting missionaries to selected areas where they naturally elicited pro-Dutch loyalty, while Muslim activities, including education, were carefully controlled. By the 1930s Indonesia's gathering nationalistic momentum was evident, and the leaders, including Sukarno and Mohammed Hatta, were arrested and imprisoned.

When the Japanese entered the Celebes and Borneo at the beginning of 1942, they were welcomed at first as brother Asians and possible allies in the liberation cause. This attitude soon turned to one of disenchantment, but not before the Japanese had freed nationalist leaders, promoted Bahasa Indonesia as a language and formed a homeguard destined to prove exceedingly useful later when the Dutch attempted to regain power. Sukarno and Mohammed Hatta were allowed positions of authority which gave them the opportunity to encourage the national yearning for independence. Progressive Japanese defeat released more power. In March 1945, the Japanese appointed a committee to examine independence. They followed this in August the same year with an Indonesian Independence Planning Committee, with Sukarno as chairman, Hatta vice-chairman. Only one week later the Japanese surrendered. Three days afterwards, on the 17 August 1945, Sukarno and Hatta proclaimed independence.

Independence

Indonesia had announced itself a republic, but Holland, long isolated from reliable, up-to-date information about events within the country, could hardly be expected to credit this as a *fait accompli*. The British made their second appearance in the islands, performing a holding operation for the Dutch. Misunderstanding of the situation, rather than ill will, resulted in fighting, including the famous Battle of Surabaya which left Indonesia itself and the world at large shaken by the intensity of nationalistic feelings. Negotiations between the Dutch and the Indonesians twice came up with partnership treaties, each time followed by Dutch so-called "police action". Finally the United Nations Security Council intervened. World opinion stood against Holland which was, in any case, spending well beyond its means on the struggle. On 27 December 1949 the Dutch transferred sovereignty, and on 17 August 1950 the new republic was officially proclaimed.

Sukarno was a charismatic figure, undeniably "father of his country". He was, naturally, opposed to capitalism and imperialism which, in his terms, boiled down to being at odds with the West. He had pronounced Marxist leanings and proved an inept economist. As well as having to balance strong groups such as religious parties, the P.K.I. (Communist party), and the army, he had to handle domestic uprisings in various areas of the new nation. Not all the islands were willing to be part of the republic—trouble still flares up periodically. His eventual failure at juggling internal politics gave rise to the attempted Communist coup of 1965. Power went to General Suharto, Sukarno was tactfully engineered into the background and, at the cost of tremendous bloodshed and anguish, the army broke and suppressed the Communist party.

Sukarno's stirring far-sightedness in early years assures him of an outstanding place in Indonesian history in spite of a totalitarian streak and errors of judgement. Quietly-spoken Suharto saw to it that his

Drying rice in Lombok. Cultivation and preparation are communal activities.

predecessor's retreat was respectfully dealt with. He became Acting President and then President in 1969. Sukarno died in 1970. Suharto's "New Order" government encourages Western investment, but technological advances have to be carefully geared to suit the needs of an emerging nation. He has made strides in curtailing the corruption which had been widespread in Indonesia long before independence.

Economy

Once topping the world for rice imports, Indonesia is now basically self-sufficient. Areas of extremely fertile volcanic soil produce rubber, soya, sugar, palm-oil, tea, coffee, cacao, bananas, copra and spices. Cool-climate fruit and vegetables flourish in the higher areas; elsewhere tropical fruits abound. Sea fishing, where the harvest is potentially great, is backed up by lake and river fishing

> ### The Five Principles
> *Indonesia's state philosophy is summarized by the* Pancasila *or Five Principles depicted symbolically on the nation's coat of arms. Belief in one God is represented by the central star; the unity of mankind by a closed chain with square links for men, round for women. The* banteng *(buffalo) stands for national unity, while the banyan tree, whose closely entwining roots give solidarity and strength, symbolizes rule by the people, which here takes the form of village democracy under a head man. Rice and cotton, meaning food and clothing for all, represent the fifth principle of social justice. The shield itself, bearing the national colours, red and white, signifies protection and the right to self-defence, with the transverse bar representing the equator.*
>
> *The coat of arms is supported by a garuda, or golden eagle, Vishnu's mount in Hindu beliefs and a sacred bird in Javanese tradition. It is always shown with 17 feathers on each outstretched wing, 8 tail feathers and 45 breast feathers, symbolizing 17 August 1945, the date of the Proclamation of Independence. The national motto, held in the garuda's claws, is* Bhinneka Tunggal Ika *("They are many, they are one"), usually translated as Unity in Diversity.*

and fish farming. Indonesia's vast rainforests, primarily in Sumatra and Kalimantan, once provided over half the world's supplies. In 1983 a huge fire wreaked havoc in East Kalimantan, and the country is now alerted to the need to protect a tropical forest zone second only to that of the Amazon.

Although 63 per cent of the people still live on the land, industry is playing an increasing part in the economy. Indonesia is the world's leading exporter of liquefied natural gas and a major producer of petroleum, tin, bauxite, nickel, copper and coal. Chemical, automotive, textile, food processing and aviation industries have grown rapidly in importance, with automobiles being exported and aircraft manufacture well established at Bandung in West Java. The country is essentially wealthy, but income distribution is highly inequitable. Foreign investment is encouraged and has been growing steadily since 1967.

In simplest terms Indonesia's aims are twofold: to retain its identity while becoming part of the modern world. The country has advanced amazingly in recent years and, with the help of its increasingly well educated, politically alert younger people, can now hope to find its own uniquely Indonesian answers to the challenges of the future.

Tipped with gold, the national monument soars over Jakarta.

WHERE TO GO

Every region of Indonesia has its own culture and attractions, ranging from historic monuments through up-market beach holidays to jungle river trips and trekking. The government is constantly developing new areas, increasing hotel accommodation, installing conference facilities for business visitors and improving roads and communications in general. Now even the remotest places are accessible, provided you're sometimes prepared to rough it. It would take months to see the whole country. Basically you have a choice of two major alternatives: in-depth exploration of a selected region, or a combination of one of the classic destinations with something more unusual. If you choose the second, plan your "adventure" trip first, leaving time to relax later at beach, lake side, or in one of the cool, high-country resorts.

If you are interested in an intensive study of culture, history, conservation or anything specific which may take you to out-of-the-way regions, get in touch with the nearest Indonesian Tourist Information Office or Diplomatic Mission in advance. Staff will tell you how to contact national bodies such as the Nature Conservation Service or the Indonesian Institute of Sciences, where there are people knowledgeable about your subject and eager to help and advise.

Wherever you go, you'll meet friendly people anxious to greet you. "Hullo Mister, Hullo Missus, where you from?" is the call sign of Indonesia.

Finding Your Way

The following words will be an invaluable help in reading maps and understanding street directions.

barat	*west*
bukit	*hill*
danau	*lake*
gereja	*church*
gunung	*mountain*
istana	*palace*
jalan *(abbr.* jl.*)*	*street*
jembatan	*bridge*
kali	*river*
kampong	*village*
kawah	*crater*
kebun	*garden*
lapangan	*square*
laut	*sea*
merdan	*square*
pantai	*beach*
pasar	*market*
pulau	*island*
puncak	*mountain*
rumah	*house*
selatan	*south*
stanplatz	*bus/taxi station*
stasiun	*railway station*
sungai	*river*
timur	*east*
utara	*north*

There's modern transport on Madura, along with a number of original alternatives.

JAVA

This island has the densest agricultural population in the world. It's the political and financial centrepoint of Indonesia with a landscape as minutely beautiful as batik, a blending of banana groves, rice fields and tea plantations thriving on the rich red volcanic soil. The administrative centre for Java, as for the whole archipelago, is Jakarta.

JAKARTA

Indonesia's capital is a sprawling, noisy metropolis of 8 million people, rapidly expanding in every direction under a heavy sky, steamy hot and metallic grey. The population is composed of dozens of ethnic groups, resulting in a huge diversity of religious beliefs, style of dress, physical characteristics and customs. It's true that Jakarta has its problems, but don't be put off—its history dates back at least 2,000 years, and the city has come a long way since then. Although the outskirts have retained

the air of a conglomeration of villages, central Jakarta is rapidly shooting skyward. The dusty, difficult city has been planted with trees; sculptured shrubbery sets off banks and hotels; multitudes of satellite TV receptors add a surrealist touch. Even the naïve nationalistic statuary of Sukarno's time has taken on a certain weathered charm. Jakarta, that erstwhile shanty town, unreal mixture of wealth and poverty, sophistication and survival, is intent on constructing a new, youthful personality without losing the underlying warmth of the old. Shining over it, landmark and symbolic lodestar, is the gold flame of the Monas, monument to independence.

Referred to by the Indonesians as *Ibu Kota* (Mother Town), Jakarta sprang up on a plain in northern Java at the mouth of the Ciliwung River, winning importance as an Asian trading port under the name of Sunda Kelapa: *Sunda* for the Hindu princes from the west Javanese kingdom of that name who controlled it for 300 years; *kelapa* for the coconut palms which graced its shores. Early in the 16th century, a Sunda prince established a treaty with the Portuguese who were already installed in the spice islands of the Moluccas and openly eyeing the riches of Java. However, this Hindu attempt to keep neighbouring Islamic states at bay was unsuccessful. On 22 June 1527, the Muslim prince Fatahillah swept in from the sultanate of Bantam (now Banten), took the port and called it Jayakarta, "Complete Victory". Under the leadership of Jan Pieterszoon Coen, the Dutch captured and razed the city in 1619; from the ruins they built Batavia, which soon became the flourishing capital of the Dutch East Indies. Within their solid fortifying walls, the Dutch dreamt of creating the Amsterdam of the tropics, building a network of canals and substantial tile-roofed houses which they filled with memories of their faraway homeland. But sanitation was poor, the canals stagnated, and European trading ships brought malaria; Batavia became the "graveyard of Dutchmen", where the annual death toll often overshot the number of living residents. Gin and pipe-smoking were considered effective preventive medicine. Captain Cook drily observed that the only member of his crew who didn't succumb to illness was a 70-year-old who stayed drunk the whole time in port.

In the early 1800s the city extended further south to more healthy areas. Colonial rule came to an end during World War II, when the Japanese occupied Indonesia. Independence was declared on 17 August 1945 and the city renamed Jakarta, a shortened form of Jayakarta. In 1949 the city was proclaimed capital of the new Republic of Indonesia.

Historical Jakarta

Start where the city was born, at the port still called **Sunda Kelapa**. The superb, tall-masted *pinisi*, many of them at least fifty years old, are built by the Buginese people of South Sulawesi in tropical hardwood to withstand knocks against coral reefs; the colour of the hull denotes ownership. They ply to the islands with necessities like soap, flour, sugar and cement, returning gunwhale-deep with a cargo of precious timbers, mostly from Sumatra and Kalimantan. Pacify your seafaring instincts by asking to explore aboard; you can also enquire about a passage to other islands. There are plenty of small craft offering **harbour tours**—worthwhile if you're a boat-lover, for this is one of the world's largest and last grand sailing fleets.

Pasar Ikan (the fish market) is close to the harbour. Even if you miss the fish auction, held at first light, it's still worth a visit. There are shells and corals as well as old-fashioned, rust-spotted anchors, coils of tarry rope, chain, sailcloth and everything to make childhood tales of the salty seas come flooding back—until the smell brings you down to earth. For escape to less odiferous surroundings, drop into the **Museum Bahari** (Marine Museum, closed Mondays) occupying old warehouses on Jl. Pasar Ikan where the Dutch stocked pepper, coffee, tea and textiles. It has a collection of marine equipment and maps. The harbourmaster's **lookout tower** near the museum offers an excellent view but you have to ask permission to enter.

27

Old Batavia was originally protected by a wall and moat, and its site is still referred to as the *kota* (fort). On your way down, keep an eye out for a beautifully skeletal restored drawbridge known as the **Chicken Market Bridge** over Kali Besar, the "Great Canal".

At the centre of the old city lies **Taman Fatahillah**, a quiet cobbled square containing the former town hall, built in 1710, now the **Museum Kota** (City Museum). It served as a prison as well as house of justice, and some cruelly imaginative tortures went on there. Prince Diponegoro, son of the sultan of Yogyakarta, was imprisoned in the dungeon in 1830 after launching an attack on the Dutch and being tricked into capitulation. The museum provides an excellent insight into the history of Jakarta, with a collection of maps, paintings—including a portrait of Governor General Coen—and objects excavated near the city. Most of the dark, solid-looking furniture was made in Java or on the Coromandel coast of India to Dutch design. Note the monument recalling the "loathsome memory" of Pieter Erbervelt, a Eurasian condemned to death in 1722 for collaborating with the Indonesians to overthrow the Dutch. To complete his dishonour, building was forbidden on the site of his house near the Portuguese Church (see p. 30) where a restored plaque names him as "traitor".

Leaving this sobering reminder of Jakarta's past, glance upwards to the late 18th-century bell which tolled the many doleful but occasionally joyful moments in the city's colonial history. Directly in front of the City Museum is **Si Jagur** (Mr Strong), a bronze cannon whose barrel terminates in a clenched fist, the Javanese symbol of virility. Childless women used to make offerings to Si Jagur and then sit on top in the hope of bearing offspring. Legend relates that a Sunda prime minister and his wife were both turned into cannons after the king gave them the hopeless task of producing such weapons. The male ended up in Batavia, while the female is kept securely locked up within the sultan's palace grounds at Solo, where she, too, is presented with offerings. In fact, Si Jagur is a perfectly normal 17th-century Portuguese cannon; its Latin inscription, *Ex me ipsa renata sum* ("From my own self am I reborn") refers to its recasting from an earlier model.

Museum Wayang, to the left of the town hall, is a fairly recent structure on the site of the old Dutch church and graveyard, where the governor generals, including Coen, were buried. Inside is a lavish display of wooden and parchment puppets. Performances, often by nationally reputed puppet masters, are held Sundays at 10 a.m. On the east side of the square is **Balai Seni Rupa** (Museum of Fine Arts), housed in the former Court of Justice built in 1870. As well as paintings and sculpture, it contains a very fine ceramics collection.

Chinese merchants attracted to Batavia were victims of a massacre in 1740 and the community was moved west, outside the city walls, to the area known as **Glodok**. This Indonesian Chinatown has been modernized, though there are still some vestiges of the past. It's difficult for vehicles to enter, so leave your taxi at Glodok Plaza and continue on foot to Jl. Kemenangan, near the Petak Sembilan market. Alongside is the mid-17th-century Chinese temple complex known as

Traditional temples throughout Indonesia are honoured by the large Chinese population.

Wihara Dharma Bhakti (Temple of Devotion to the Law). The interior glows richly red and gold, with joss sticks wafting heady incense. Note the two 18th-century lions guarding the main building where porcelain figures decorate the roof. In the courtyard, where small birds are released to bring good luck, you can have your fortune told. You'll be made welcome and are free to wander around; ask permission if you'd like to take photographs. Much of the area has become commercial, few other old Chinese buildings survive, but there are plenty of oriental restaurants, shops, and an entertainment centre.

East of Batavia, at Jl. Pangeran Jayakarta 1, stands **Gereja Sion**, the Portuguese Church. It was constructed between 1693 and 1695 by the Dutch as a place of worship for the many Eurasians, some of part-Portuguese origin, who were released from slavery on the condition that they converted to the Dutch Reformed Church. Known as *Mardijkers,* they flourished to form a wealthy social class. The bell outside, cast in Batavia, comes from an earlier structure. Inside are carved ebony pews, a splendid 17th-century baroque pulpit, copper chandeliers and many memorials to prominent people.

Central Jakarta

There's no missing **Medan Merdeka** (Freedom Square), the vast open heart of Jakarta, surrounded by official buildings. It used to be a military training ground and, before that, pastureland for animals. The famous **Monas** (National Monument) towers above it, an Italian marble obelisk 110 m (360 ft) tall, with the Torch of Independence gleaming at the top. Thirty-five kg (77 lb) of gold leaf were used for the flame, which houses the lift engine. Pause in the

Hall of Independence to see dioramas of Indonesian history, before taking the lift to the top for a great view of the city. The monument's base commemorates Independence Day (17 August 1945). Near the main entrance, the dashing equestrian statue honours Prince Diponegoro, 19th-century freedom fighter.

West on Medan Merdeka is the **National Museum**, also referred to as Museum Pusat (Central). This neoclassical building, constructed 1862–68, is the third to contain the collection of the Batavian Society for Arts and Sciences, the oldest and one of the most prestigious learned bodies in South-East Asia, founded in 1778. The bronze elephant outside was presented by the king of Siam in 1871 in exchange for objects from Borobudur. On the ground floor are the archaeological, ethnographic and ceramics departments with Hindu-Buddhist objects recalling Indonesia's early trade relationship with India and the religions and literature it brought in its wake. Note the gentle, meditative smile of some of the carved faces, not unlike that on archaic Greek statues and seen again on the great Buddhas at Borobudur. The staggering display of **Oriental porcelain** is one of the largest and most valuable outside China. The 5,000 pieces represent the collection of Egbert Willem van Orsey de Flines, who donated it to the museum provided he could be its curator, which he was until 1959.

The **treasure room** upstairs exhibits gold objects, including a superb 22-carat necklace from Banda Aceh, North Sumatra, ornate gold and bamboo flutes from Bali, krises, and a collection of weapons from various islands. If time presses, concentrate on the Hindu-Buddhist and ceramics displays but on no account miss the treasure. The museum is closed all day Monday. There's a tour in English at 9.30 a.m. on Tuesday, Wednesday, Thursday and every last Sunday in the month, led by an enthusiastic member of the Ganesha Volunteers' Group.

Eye-catching for its modernity and huge white dome, **Istiqlal Mosque** stands on the north-east corner of the square on Jl. Veteran. It was one of Sukarno's most cherished projects and is one of the biggest mosques in South-East Asia, opened in 1978 by President Suharto. Visitors are welcome provided they avoid prayer times and observe the requisite courtesies. Across the road on Jl. Kathedral, a small, neo-Gothic Catholic **cathedral**, ebulliently and unmistakably proclaiming its Art Nouveau origins, shoots openwork spires into the sky.

Near the present-day Borobudur Hotel, **Lapangan Banteng** developed from malarial swamp to become a centrepiece for Dutch life, highlighted by three buildings: the White House, a 19th-century administrative palace, now the Department of Commerce; the Supreme Court; and the former

> ### Talking Shop
> All round Jakarta you'll run across specialized street markets, stalls, or individual hawkers proffering everything from goldfish to bottled water, from rattan furniture to herbal remedies and prickly, aphrodisiac durian fruit.
>
> If you're into collecting old objects, try your buyer's luck in Jl. Surabaya, the city's flea market. Things aren't what they used to be, but connoisseurs still have their lucky days. Possible finds include Delft porcelain, old Dutch coins and oil lamps, Chinese objects and some fine traditional pieces from all the Indonesian islands.
>
> Bird-lovers have a mixed reaction to pasar burung, the bird markets on Jl. Pramuka, almost directly west of the flea market. There are avenues of birds cawing, carolling and flapping in a cacophony of sound and a continuous shower of birdseed. This is the place for a close-up of the perkutut, a small, softly coloured songbird which is a status symbol and costs a minor fortune. The Javanese swing perkutut cages high up in front of their homes and hold local singing competitions for the inmates.

masonic lodge "The Star in the East", now a pharmacy. On this square you'll see the huge figure of The Chainbreaker, recalling Independence in Irian Jaya.

Emmanuel Church on Jl. Merdeka Timur, originally called

31

Willemskirk after Willem I of the Netherlands, was completed in 1839 for the Dutch Protestant community. The architect, J. H. Horst, conceived it in romanticized Greco-Roman style—you almost expect to glimpse nymphs and shepherds among the congregation, which is seated around a central pulpit. A sagaciously planned dome floods the interior with limpid light. The church houses several rare ecclesiastical objects including a Dutch Bible dated 1748 and an almost unique 19th-century Dutch organ which replaced the military band that once provided music. Superb acoustics make it the venue for many concerts. To the south-east, the Anglican **All-Saints Church,** erected by the British in 1829, has hand-painted windows from a World War II prison chapel, and a grave-

---

The Art of Batik

Batik can indicate status, bring good luck or placate the spirits. It appears to date back to the 16th century, although similar processes were used long before that in Egypt and elsewhere.

The best batik comes from Java. The word refers to the process as well as the resultant printed cloth, which is usually cotton, sometimes linen or silk. Yogyakarta and Solo remain major suppliers of top-quality fabric, recognizable because of its insistence on brown, cream and indigo.

The pattern is achieved by applying melted beeswax to the cloth to create dye-resistant areas. For tulis *batik the design is hand-drawn with a* canting, *a small tool with bamboo handle and metal spout; for* cap *batik a copper stamp—often a work of art in itself—is dipped in the wax then pressed on to the fabric. Most batik nowadays is produced by this more commercial method: you can easily differentiate the two as* tulis *batik has no wrong side,* cap *batik does. Once the first colour is applied, the wax is boiled and scraped off, reapplied to another area and the fabric re-dipped in another dye. This process can be repeated many times. Chemical dyes are now common but you can still find hand-drawn fabric coloured with natural dyes—at a price.*

The normal width is 102 cm (40 in). Stock sizes are the kain panggang, *two-and-a-half times the width; the* dodot, *four times the width; and the* sarung, *usually stitched down the side to become cylindrical, twice the width. The* slendang, *a kind of scarf, is worn across the shoulder by women. Men wear headgear called* kain kepala. *Batik clothing is nearly always considered good taste; a batik long-sleeved shirt is normal semi-formal evening wear for men.*

Before you start investing, study the treasures in the Jakarta Central Museum or visit the Jakarta Textile Museum on Jl. Satsuit Tuban. What you finally buy may have come from a small factory (which you can visit to observe the dyeing processes) or from thousands of cottage workers around the country.

yard evocative of times past.

Taman Ismail Marzuki, otherwise known as TIM, is the municipal art centre with two galleries, one for graphics and one for contemporary art, a planetarium and a comprehensive programme of cultural events. The monthly programme is available at the box office, at the Visitor's Centre, and at most hotels.

On the west side of the city, the **Textile Museum** on Jl. Satsuit Tubun is a prime place to study the multitudinous kinds of batik and weaving both ancient and modern. There's an excellent library, a collection of old photographs, a display of textile-making equipment and a workshop.

Wayang characters from Hindu epics provide inspiration for many crafts, including batik.

Around the City

At **Ragunan Zoo**, in a suburb 16 km (10 miles) south of the centre of Jakarta, the stars are the "dragons" from Komodo Island. Fully grown, these reptiles are capable of crunching up a whole goat—or a person. These small, but far from pint-sized, examples make do with chickens. Usually they're more interested in snoozing than in showing off. Shared top billing goes to the birds of paradise from Irian Jaya.

Just off the toll motorway to Bogor, stretching over 120 ha (296 acres), is **Taman Mini Indonesia**, one of Jakarta's exceptional attractions. It aims at displaying the whole country in miniature with a succession of pavilions representing the various provinces and their culture. To brush up on your geography, take a cablecar over the artificial lake shaped like a map of Indonesia. Taman Mini seems to have everything—a good museum, buildings for the Islamic, Protestant Christian, Catholic, Hindu and Buddhist faiths, an orchid garden, restaurants, horse-drawn carts or buses for getting around, even a replica of Borobudur Temple and, in the open-plan aviary, a jet-black *beo* bird that whistles the national anthem—provided you give it the starting note!

At Pondok Gede, 3 km (2 miles) east of Taman Mini, is Jakarta's most

Glittering costumes, clowning, music: all part of the show in Mini Indonesia.

memorable monument, **Pancasila Cakti**, usually known as Lubang Buaya (Crocodile Hole). It was raised in honour of six generals and an officer murdered during the attempted Communist coup of 1965. The uniformed figures point dramatically towards the well into which their bodies were thrown.

For the ultimate recreational experience, visit **Taman Impian Jaya Ancol** (Ancol Dreamland) on the waterfront between Sunda Kelapa and the modern port of Tanjung Priok. Apart from a huge swimming pool, golf, bowling, an oceanarium with performing dolphins, a racing circuit and beach facilities, there's also an excellent craft bazaar. On Sundays, when the park gets very crowded, there are performances by Javanese dancers, giant puppets and clowns. The latest addition is the Fantasy Land theme park.

East of the pleasure grounds, rather hard to find (ask for Jl. Pantai Sanur), the 17th-century Chinese temple known as **Klenteng Ancol** is revered by two groups, the Chinese and the Muslims.

Boats set out from Ancol Marina to Pulau Seribu, the lovely islands of the Java Sea.

Pulau Seribu

These "Thousand Islands" provide Jakarta with an ocean escape route. In fact there are about 600, of which only seven are populated; the rest are frequented only by seabirds, would-be Robinson Crusoes and fishermen, who catch "long tom" or garfish with a loop of string and a kite. The diving and fishing are marvellous, and beginning to attract an international crowd.

Bidadari is the closest, consequently the most crowded. Further out, gloriously set in clear tropical waters, lies the group called **Pulau Seribu Paradise**, of which Pulau Putri is a long-standing favourite, followed by its sister islands, Pelangi, Perak, and Papa Theo, a diver's idea of submarine heaven. Petundan offers luxury accommodation, and Sepak is for groups. On **Pulau Putri**, pay your respects to the giant lizards. They waddle up to the kitchen door for scraps and grow over 120 cm (4 ft) long with a girth to match. A number of islets are nature reserves, ideal for picnics and diving. The flaming tropical sunsets are memorable, with bats flitting home along the beach.

Inter-island transport is by *perahu* (single-masted sailboat), although there's a launch available, too. Weekdays are cheapest for the islands. If you take a bungalow with kitchen, bring your own food. For full information about boat, plane, helicopter transport, call in to the Pulau Seribu Paradise office, Jakarta Theatre Building, Jl. Thamrin 9.

WEST JAVA

The plains and mountains of West Java are luxuriantly green, nourished by the fertile soil from a number of volcanoes. Excluding Jakarta, which is autonomous, the province covers 46,300 sq km (7,877 sq miles) and is historically known as Sunda. The Sundanese have their own language (related to Sanskrit) and their own traditional arts, which include *angklung* music with bamboo instruments, *wayang golek* (doll puppets), and a style of dancing admired for its sensuous grace.

Old stones inscribed in Sanskrit and found near Bogor mention Taruma, a 5th-century Hindu kingdom ruled by Purnavarman, who planned a canal to link Bekasi, near the north coast, to the port of Sunda Kelapa. Taruma was taken over by the Buddhist Srivijaya kingdom from South Sumatra and then the Hindu Mataram in Central Java. Centuries later, the trade-conscious Hindu Pajajaran dynasty reigned, developed commerce with outside nations, settled Sunda Kelapa as a trading spot and made a treaty with the Portuguese. When the Islamic Banten army triumphed in the 16th century, many noble Pajajaran fled to remote areas where, today, their descendants are believed to form part of the Badui people who live in isolation from the rest of the world, with "no police, no money, not much government".

Temperatures vary from around 14°C (57°F) in the misty mountains near Puncak to a sizzling 35°C (95°F) or more on the coast. Jakarta gives easy access to the province for day trips and longer tours. Banten possesses its share of romantic ruins and can be a starting-point for the magnificent western beaches; Ujung Kulon National Park on the farthest westerly tip is a prime nature reserve. One of the most rewarding trips is cross-country through Bogor and the Puncak Pass to Bandung, capital of West Java, then via Garut to Tasikmalaya and Pangandaran, which figure among the best beaches in Indonesia, near another, more accessible, forest reserve.

The Banten Area

The Bantenese kingdom was long a thorn in the side of the Dutch who regarded it as one of the most rebellious parts of the archipelago. Dutch ships anchored first at Banten in 1596 before conquering the rest of the islands. They found an exciting and wealthy port where Indians, Chinese, Turks, Persians, Arabs and Sundanese rubbed shoulders in a market crammed with exotic silks, spices, ceramics and jewellery. Pepper was one of the prize exports. The harbour has long since silted up; by the 19th century Banten had declined into a humble fishing village.

Serang is the crossroads where you turn off for **Banten Lama** (Old Banten), some 10 km (6 miles) away. Among the ghostly remains, **Istana Kaibon**, the palace built for Queen Aisyah, the mother of Banten's last sultan, was destroyed by the Dutch governor general Daendels in 1832. Surosowan Palace, another slumbrous ruin recently excavated, stands directly opposite the Grand Mosque, **Mesjid Agung**, in Chinese pagoda style. There's a fine view of the coastline from the top of the minaret. A **museum** to the right houses a selection of antique kris handles, weapons, pottery, old bottles and clay tobacco pipes. You'll also see a selection of instruments used by local mystics in their trance rituals. Known as *debus,* this is a form of self-defence that aims at proving invulnerability to injury. Participants are cut, jabbed with spikes (like those in the museum), buried alive or suffer pots of burning coals on their heads, all apparently without pain. Ask a local travel agent about performances.

The grim outline of **Fort Speelwijk** is softened by coconut palms fluttering above chipped stone walls. The bastion was built in 1682 and abandoned in the early 19th century. You can go up one of the watchtowers for the view. A great deal more cheerful is the 200-year-old **Klenteng** (Chinese temple) opposite, with a handsome, sacred, carved chair kept out of harm's way in a glass case.

From March to August, nature-lovers can hire a boat at Banten's Karanghantu harbour for a half-hour ride to **Pulau Dua** to observe migratory birds such as mynahs, sea eagles and kingfishers that stay on this island for the mating season.

Indonesia's largest steel mill dominates the town of **Cilegon**, alleviated by up-market leisure facilities for highly paid executives. **Merak** flourishes as an industrial town and port with a large expatriate community; ferries leave about hourly for South Sumatra.

Florida Beach, only 5 km (3 miles) from Merak, consists of a succession of delightful sandy bays, peaceful during the week but inundated with crowds at weekends. The road loops south along the shoreline to **Anyer**, which was the biggest Dutch port in the area until Krakatau washed it away with a giant tidal wave. The existing Dutch lighthouse was built two years afterwards, in 1885. There are plenty of expats here, too, enjoying the excellent swimming, snorkelling and fishing. From Anyer you can hire a boat to visit lonely **Sangian Island**—swamps, jungle, wildlife, coral gardens, and a hungry crowd of mosquitoes when the sun goes down. Looming in the distance is the outline of Krakatau volcano. On **Karang Bolong** beach, a huge arch of rock frames the sea some 20 km (12 miles) from **Carita**, one of the loveliest seashores in the whole of Java, with safe swimming, cooling breezes and a gentle surf. From there it's just a hop to Labuhan, departure point for Ujung Kulon nature reserve and for Krakatau.

Krakatau

Once an attractive island 40 km (25 miles) off the West Java coast, this mighty blowhole lay quiescent for more than 200 years until 27 August 1883 when, after some three months of preparatory hiss and bubble, it let fly with the biggest natural explosion ever recorded, flinging out ash that carried all around the globe. Nearly 20 cu km (5 cu miles) of rock shot into the sky, while water rushing into the shattered vents precipitated a gigantic tidal wave that killed 36,000 people on the coasts of Java and Sumatra. A noise like cannons boomed over Singapore, beer-glasses rattled in Brisbane, debris catapulted across the Indian Ocean to Africa. For two-and-a-half days, absolute darkness reigned within a radius of 150 km (93 miles). The ash drifted several times round the world, causing violet sunsets throughout the following year. Krakatau had spoken—and in so doing it had blown itself to bits.

Decades later, in 1928, after much submarine fuss and bother, **Anak Krakatau** ("Child of Krakatau") rose above the sea from its parent's submerged caldera. The smoking cone is steadily growing, a few metres each year, and vegetation is slowly taking a foothold. Further north, **Krakatau Kecil** ("Little Krakatau") is another chip off the old block. If you do decide to drop in on this temperamental tribe, arrange the trip beforehand with a travel agent in Jakarta or on the spot in Labuhan or Carita Beach. Whether you actually get there depends on the mood of the day. Trips are not advisable unless sea conditions are stable; from April to the beginning of September is the most likely time. Make sure you get a good boat that can handle a rough crossing. Start very early to avoid the heat, and bear in mind the various hazards ashore, which can include noxious gases and showers of hot boulders. If you're fortunate in your timing you may be able to undertake the 30-minute climb to the crater—but remember that Krakatau is not to be trifled with at any time.

Ujung Kulon

Set on Java's farthest westerly tip, the Ujong Kulon peninsula is cut off from the rest of the island by a marshy isthmus. It forms a protected nature reserve together with Krakatau, the Gunung Honje massif to the east of the isthmus, and Panaitan and Pencang islands. The region was singed and coated with dust by Krakatau's explosion, but

---

A Lost Tribe

The mysterious Badui people live in the hills just south of Rangkasbitung, cut off from the rest of the world. They are said to have fled here from the Hindu city of Pajajaran (near Bogor) in the 16th century to escape Islamization, but their religion—animism with Islamic overtones—contradicts this. They believe in an ultimate deity and acknowledge Muhammad. The Javanese speak of them with a mixture of fear and respect because they are thought to have occult powers. Their herbal remedies are much sought after.

The Badui Luar ("Outer Badui") form a buffer zone encircling the three villages of the Badui Dalam ("Inner Badui"). The puun, *or spiritual leader, of each village is considered sacred; his position is hereditary. Each year he travels to Gunung Kendeng, the holy place, which is out of bounds to everyone else.*

The Inner Badui speak an archaic Sundanese dialect, go everywhere on foot, are forbidden to touch money or cut their hair and are not supposed to leave the confines of their ancestral lands. They wear white, handspun clothing. Theft, adultery and manslaughter are completely outlawed, and they are not allowed to eat four-legged animals. They do not sell their crops. In any case, food supplies are limited, for their taboos confine them to "shifting agriculture" based on clearing an area of forest for one or two seasons, then letting the jungle return and cultivating a new patch.

The Badui Luar have slightly more leeway. Clothed in dark sarongs, they control all comings and goings for the inner territory, tanah larangan. *To visit the Badui Dalam, you must first obtain permission from the Kantor Kabupaten (District Office) in Rangkasbitung. An Outer Badui will guide you on the four-day hike to Cibeo village, involving jungle tracks and river crossing. You will be completely reliant on the reactions and hospitality of the people; normally visitors are not permitted to stay there overnight.*

---

now jungle has bandaged the scars. Here, in thick forest, saline swamp and grassy clearings live *banteng* (wild ox), the Javanese tiger, mouse deer, tribes of leaf-monkeys, green peafowl and the rare, armoured white rhinoceros that Marco Polo called a unicorn. The peninsula coast has a marvellous sea-garden, but avoid the dangerous southern and western beaches.

The prime time for visiting and maybe glimpsing the cantankerous rhino is April to October. Arrange your permit at the Forestry Office near Labuhan. Accommodation is available in the reserve but you'll need to take your own food supplies.

Bogor and Vicinity

It's a comfortable ride from Jakarta to Bogor, 60 km (37 miles) south— less than an hour by car along the excellent toll highway or a little more by train. Gates mark your exit from the metropolitan area into the West Javanese countryside where women in sarongs and wide hats bend over their hoes in a minutely cultivated green and tawny landscape.

As you mount into the hills the air grows cooler, the foliage thicker, washed to sparkling brightness by almost daily downpours. "Rain City" is Bogor's second name. Dutch residents used to withdraw from insalubrious Batavia to invigorating, breezy Bogor, 290 m (950 ft) above sea-level in the foothills of Mts Gede and Salak. Horse-drawn carts trotting through the shady streets add a bucolic touch even though Bogor lies too close to Jakarta to be able to retain more than a hint of its original hill-town charm. For years it has been a research centre for botany, biology and allied sciences, centred around the famous botanical gardens.

On the road into town spreads **Istana Bogor**, the Presidential Palace, built in 1745 for Baron Gustaf Willem van Imhoff, governor general during the days of the Dutch East Indies Company. Raffles used it as a country residence when he was in Java. Reconstructed and enlarged in the 19th century, the mansion appears romantically old world, with graceful neoclassic columns lifting above sweeping lawns grazed smooth by herds of spotted deer. After Independence, Sukarno often stayed here, amassing a prestigious collection of paintings. Consent for visits is necessary in writing well in advance from the Chief of Protocol, Istana Negara, Jl. Veteran, Jakarta.

Behind the palace stretches **Kebon Raya**, the botanical garden also known as Kebon Jodoh ("Courtship Garden") because of the many couples demurely wooing in the magnificent grounds. The glorious expanse of more than 85 ha (210 acres) was dreamed up by Raffles during the short time the British administered the East Indies. The gardens opened in 1817 and contain

The old story of boy meets girl unfolds in the idyllic setting of Bogor's botanical gardens.

15,000 species, including magical orchids, forest giants from Borneo, swaying groves of bamboo and curiosities like the huge water lily, *Victoria regia*, and the monstrous Rafflesia, the biggest flower in the world, which displays its distinctly evil-smelling bloom in October. It's a good idea to hire a student guide to discover the gardens' secrets.

On Jl. Batu Tulis, see the **inscribed stone** dating from the ancient Pajajaran Kingdom; there's an even older one, dated 450 AD in **Ciampea** village. While in Bogor, drop in on the **gong foundry**, 17 Jl. Pancasan, to witness the ancient art of gamelan manufacture. This is one of the two last workshops in Indonesia; the other is in Solo.

South from Bogor, 2½ hours by car, lies the coastal fishing village of **Pelabuhanratu**. It's colourful, relaxed and unspoiled, the seafood is delicious—but don't tangle with Nyai Loro Kidul, goddess of the South Seas. At the Pesta Nelayan festival in April, the Sundanese throw flowers and a buffalo's head into the Indian Ocean at this spot, the entrance to her domain. You'll be earnestly advised by Indonesians not to wear green on southern beaches. It's *her* colour, and once you've seen the sea crashing in at **Pantai Karang Hawu**, 5 km (3 miles) to the west of Pelabuhanratu Bay, you'll agree it's better to avoid catching her eye. A room at Samudra Beach Hotel is always kept vacant for the goddess as a prudent mark of respect.

If you decide to leave this treacherous part of the coast and its watery deity for a subsequent encounter, take the road east of Bogor and wind slowly through the tea plantations to Puncak. Keep a sweater in the car, it can be chilly here. The tiny town of **Gadok** specializes in aluminium cupolas and spires for mosques and minarets. A **safari park** near Cisarua is frequented by sociable zebras, giraffes and emus and rather less congenial rhinos and tigers.

Then the road mounts higher, winding above misty valleys and tea plantations into low cloud. Stop for a tour of the tea plantation at **Gunung Mas** and walk through it to **Telega Warna**, a tri-coloured lake reflecting the hues of the sky. Once through the Puncak ("Summit") Pass, you'll reach **Cipanas**, with hot springs, a branch of the Bogor Botanical Gardens, and another delightful country mansion, originally built in 1750. This is your starting-point if you wish to climb Gunung Gede.

Bandung and Vicinity

West Java's capital city, with a population of 1¾ million the third largest after Jakarta and Surabaya, sits on a plateau 730 m (2,400 ft) above sea level, surrounded by a palisade of extinct and not-so-extinct volcanoes. During the twenties and thirties it was known as the Paris of Java, a somewhat exaggerated tribute to its Art Deco buildings and tree-lined "boulevards". Often referred to today as Kota Kembang (City of Flowers), it is more remarkable for pedicabs than parks—hundreds of *becaks* moved here when they were banned from the streets of Jakarta. Aircraft manufacture is attaining international importance; on the outskirts a swinging "jeans village" with unlikely papier-mâché shop frontages throbs to pop music. Nevertheless a pleasant provincial atmosphere lingers on, charged with intellectual excitement from the presence of the Bandung Institute of Technology (ITB). The girls are reputed the prettiest in Java but you'd have to be Solomon to justify the claim in a country where feminine beauty is the rule rather than the exception.

The flowery landscape near Leles is one of the loveliest in Java.

The Shadow World

All around the world, theatre sprang from religious ritual, and in Indonesia the two are still inseparable. Wayang ("ghost" or "shadow") performances are offered for occasions such as circumcision, marriage and childbirth, to ward off evil, induce a good rice crop, bring rain or welcome a friend after a long journey. The players are usually puppets, directed by a dalang. *Monarch of the shadow world, he acts as priest as much as performer, and is an important figure in his village. He possesses manifold skills in puppet-handling, ventriloquism, language and dramatic understanding, and may carve his own marionettes. The language used is Javanese or Sundanese and, on occasion, Archaic Javanese.*

Wayang kulit, *the most popular form, started some 2,000 years ago and probably grew out of ancestor worship. Existing legends were embroidered with tales from the Hindu epics, the* Mahabharata *and the* Ramayana; *Islam, in turn, added Arabian elements. But all sorts of ingredients are grist to the mill—Christianity, the struggle against the Dutch, Independence, politicians, local gossip.*

The stylized, filigree buffalo-parchment puppets are painted in bright colours and liberally gilded, even though the audience sees only the shadow. Children like to dodge around the back to watch the dalang *at work. His frail shadows strut and fret on the screen, not for an hour but usually all night, to the delighted whoops and yells or intaken awestruck breaths of the audience which, of course, knows the basic story backwards. You'll hear* wayang kulit *on the radio, too. It's even available on cassette, not as a tourist item but because the Javanese really do find it compulsive listening.*

Wayang golek *developed out of* wayang kulit *with the introduction of doll puppets from China, but since it came later it has more Islamic elements. Its home territory is West Java. More down-to-earth than the flickering, symbolic* kulit, *it is often presented during the day.*

Wayang topeng *presents stories of court intrigue mimed by masked male dancers who either speak their lines or have them spoken by a* dalang. *In* wayang wong *the heavily made-up "human puppets" perform in profile, imitating* wayang kulit. *There is dialogue, exquisite costuming, but no masks, except for dancers playing animal roles. It's an extraordinary example of nature imitating art, real people acting as much as possible like the adored flat leather marionettes.*

Wayang *is art and religion, morality as well as entertainment. The figures move and act in a prescribed way, and even the finest often have a fatal flaw. Particularly beloved are the* panakawan, *clowns and dwarves whose understanding of humanity is so broad they challenge even the gods. It's all an exceedingly subtle business and if you follow it a little you'll have better insight into the highly charged background of the Javanese.*

Dutch visitors wax nostalgic over the city's older buildings, some rather the worse for wear. At **Gedung Merdeka** (Freedom Building) Indonesia made history with the Afro-Asia conference in 1955, the basis for the present day's non-aligned movement, comprising mostly Third World countries. Constructed in 1895, it is open in the morning when you can visit the museum. **Gedung Sate**, the Provincial Administrative and Telecommunications Centre on Jl. Diponegoro, shows a nice twenties flair. Visit the **Geological Museum**, housed nearby in the former Dutch Geological Service headquarters, for fossils, rocks, and inside information on what makes a volcano tick (open mornings except Sunday). The city's reputation for Art Deco architecture is borne out by the **Savoy Homann Hotel**, though recent restoration has somewhat modified the volumes, planned to have the sweep of a transatlantic liner.

Sukarno first drew attention for nationalist activities during his student days at the **ITB**, Indonesia's top university, opened in 1920 and often compared to MIT. Indicative of Indonesia's decisive advance into the technological age, the university has a formidable reputation for producing leaders. In Minangkabau style, the complex is endowed with a pleasant campus and lively-minded students, eager to inform, expound, discuss and make friends in several languages.

Bandung supplies most of the world's quinine, and visitors are welcome to learn about it at the **Quinine Factory**; on Jl. Jeneral Achmad Yani the **Textile Research** and **Ceramics institutes** both offer free tours.

The Sundanese make marvellous wooden puppets for the *wayang golek* theatre. You can visit a **workshop** off Kebon Kawung (take Jl. Akbar and turn into Jl. Umar at the back of the sports grounds), and watch a performance, held at 9 p.m. every Saturday in Gedung Yayasan Pusat Kebudayan, Jl. Naripan. The **Konservatori Karawitan**, Jl. Buahbatu, is the place for Sundanese dance and music. Justifiably a big hit with visitors, **Pak Ujo's school**, 118 Jl. Padasuka, presents *wayang golek* and dancing each afternoon from 3 p.m. by heart-winning youngsters, as well as an *angklung* ensemble. The *angklung* is an instrument made of mounted bamboo tubes that produces sounds like an aerial zither, particularly effective as accompaniment to the *suling*, the Sunda flute whose sweet, wailing notes Indonesians compare to the weeping of a princess or a singing bird.

Bandung's **markets** for flowers (*pasar bunga*) and birds (*pasar waringen*) and **zoo** all offer retreat from what has become a bustling, traffic-laden city. For a sunset view, go up to the **Dago Teahouse** north of the city, run by students from ITB.

Bandung's real appeal exists in the high country around. Only 16 km

(10 miles) north, pretty little **Lembang**, a sports-minded hill resort with marigolds and poinsettias flaring in all the gardens, boasts a superb fruit and vegetable market. **Maribayo** hot springs lie just east, right beside **Sukarandeg** where, on Sunday mornings, the entertainment is ram fights, visitors welcome, bets accepted. Put two rams together and the one that butts the hardest wins. You'll wince as you watch but it's not a fight to the finish—both dazed participants usually survive to clash skulls another day.

Bandung is located on the bed of an ancient lake, formed when **Tangkuban Prahu** ("Overturned Canoe") volcano erupted, only to drain away again after the mountain changed its mind and let fly with another explosion. There are about ten craters, one of which, **Kawah Ratu**, is accessible by car and currently dormant. It's a steep and sometimes slippery climb down through forest to look into **Kawah Domas**. In the early morning, you may sight monkeys along the trail. The crater is still bubbling away in a series of boiling mud pools and sulphur vents. If you go down to look inside, remember that all thermal areas are potentially dangerous—a crust of earth may cover a lethal crack in the ground, and there is an added risk from

Thermal areas demand respect as well as admiration. Indonesia is on the Pacific ring of fire.

fumes. The mountain, which last erupted in 1969, is under constant seismic surveillance. Nearby, **Ciater** hot springs are said to be good for rheumatic disorders and skin complaints and provide a fine place to relax after your exertions. Ciater tea estate offers a fascinating tour and a great view over the surrounding area. **Jatiluhur Lake**, on the site of a vast hydro-electric project near Purwakarta, is ideal for boating, swimming and water-skiing in addition to tennis, and does not attract too many tourists.

In **Ciwidey**, south-west of Bandung, smiths make iron implements using primitive bamboo bellows and charcoal furnaces. **Pengalengan** has tea plantations and picture-postcard countryside. From there it's 15 km (9 miles) to **Mt Papandayan** which last blew its top in 1772, killing almost 3,000 people; it remains unmistakably active.

The road east of Bandung to Garut, drowsing in a gentle landscape of glinting paddy fields, passes through **Leles**. Here the countryside is unforgettably lovely. The road to **Candi Cangkuang**, a Hindu temple 2 km (a good mile) from Leles, winds between fishponds and great drifts of pale pink waterlilies with dragonflies hovering like blue needles. Occasional pony carts spank by under giant jackfruit trees, bells and harness jingling and sparkling in the sunlight. The sense of unreality continues when you hire a long bamboo raft comfortably equipped with low cane seating to be poled across a placid lake to the 9th-century temple. It's tiny, a mere dot compared with the giants Prambanan and Borobudur, but set in delightful gardens with a track meandering through the nearby village into the fields.

Midway between Garut and Tasikmalaya (watch out on the left for a narrow right-of-way), **Naga** traditional village stretches in a valley at the foot of 300 steps which seem double the number when you have to toil back up. Built almost entirely of stone, it's an isolated, introspective place, but the villagers appear unperturbed as they lead you through the maze of dark, pebbled lanes to appreciate their daily life, or when you watch them harvest the rice, blade by careful blade.

After Tasikmalaya, reputed for rattan articles and floral batik, the road runs via Banjar to **Pangandaran**, an alluring white-sand beach area, particularly popular with the younger set. Pangandaran Nature Reserve hangs offshore like a ripe fruit bobbing in the Indian Ocean, with the narrow isthmus where Pangandaran township is sited as the stalk. East is the fishing village and market, a great place for meeting up with locals but not recommended for swimming. The safest bathing stretches south on the west beach— clean sand, clear sea and a protective coral reef. At **Pasir Putih** the jealous goddess of the South Seas seems positively docile, but it is still her domain and she is honoured every December with a festival. Back along the coastline towards **Cijulang**, where an airport is planned, are two swimming lagoons; surf can be high at Batu Hiu and Batu Karas.

The nature reserve is easily accessible and you can walk through it or take a jeep. Composed of thick forest, it is inhabited by *banteng,* porcupine, deer, monkeys and birds—nothing particularly dangerous. Hire a local guide and take the jungle in your stride.

Many visitors travel by boat from **Kalipucang**, a little north-east of Pangandaran, voyaging through mangrove swamps to Cilacap in Central Java.

Cirebon

Few foreigners visit Cirebon, yet it's of historic interest as the place where Hindu and Islamic interests came to blows in the 15th century and as the seat of a once powerful sultanate. Indonesians call it Kota Udang ("Shrimp City") because of its seafood. The most attractive route runs through Bandung (131 km, 81 miles), but the rather dull northern coastal route from Jakarta is faster.

Visit the **royal cemetery** on the main Jakarta road, containing the tomb of Sunan Gunung Jati, one of the 9 *wali* (religious leaders) who spread Islam in Java. Two old *kraton* or sultans' palaces, the **Kasepuhan** and the **Kanoman**, have museums, each with an amazing royal carriage

among a number of other, rather dilapidated objects. One, bound to make you regret this age of motorized transport, is in the shape of a winged elephant. **Masjid Agung** (the Grand Mosque), with a two-tiered roof in a style typical of Balinese architecture, is almost entirely of wood and dates from around 1500. **Taman Sunyaragi**, 4 km (2$^1/_2$ miles) southeast of the city, is a pleasure palace built by Sunan Gunung Jati for his Chinese wife, then restored by a Chinese architect in the 19th century. The result is a maze of tunnels and secret doors—you almost expect a Disneyland dragon to bat its wings at the end of a labyrinth.

Cirebon is one place where you might run across increasingly rare *wayang topek* (mask dances, see page 44). The local batik using a traditional, Chinese-influenced motif of rocks and clouds is exceptionally good. The best is made at **Trusmi**, 5 km (3 miles) to the west. Chinese influence is also evident in carved jade, ivory and lacquerwork.

CENTRAL JAVA

Today's sultans hold no power outside their courts, yet you'll sense immediately you visit the royal palaces that this is the compelling and powerfully mystic homeland of Javanese culture. Islam first became implanted at Demak, in the north, and the Grand Mosque there remains a holy place for Muslims. Much older temples recall the Hindu and Buddhist

---

Festivals in Central Java

Check your Calendar of Events for the following:

Seketan. *Held during the week preceding Muhammad's birthday, this festival was originally intended to attract people to the mosque. In Yogya and Solo, two sets of sacred gamelan instruments are carried from the sultan's palace to the Grand Mosque and played there for seven days, Thursday night and Friday morning excepted. The Prophet's birthday and some other festivals are honoured by parading huge ceremonial food mounds (gunungan) which are blessed at the mosque and distributed. Both Yogya and Solo hold a fair in front of the mosque.*

Labuhan. *Annual offering to Nyi Roro Kidul, the goddess of the South Sea (Indian Ocean) coinciding in Central Java with the sultan's birthday. Similar rituals are held at the crests of the Merapi and Lawu volcanoes.*

Sendangsano Pilgrimage. *Every May there's a Catholic pilgrimage to the spring of Dendangosono in the Menoreh mountains, 32 km (20 miles) north-west of Yogyakarta. Thousands of candles are lit to a statue of the Virgin Mary.*

Yaqowiyu. *A local "pancake day" in the village of Jatinom, 20 km (12 miles) west of Solo. Pancakes are tossed from a tower. If you manage to obtain a bit, you're supposed to have good luck.*

---

dynasties of the 8th to 10th centuries; these philosophies, too, are deeply imbedded in Central Javanese belief. The main port is Cilacap; Semarang, the provincial capital, also has a busy harbour. However, the spiritual capitals are Yogyakarta and Solo. This is the most densely populated administrative area in Indonesia, with most of the people working on the land. Sometimes older people will greet you not in Bahasa but in High Javanese. Tread gently—you are in the world of traditions, dreams, and symbols.

Semarang and Vicinity

The route east from Cirebon runs through towns celebrated for their crafts. **Tegal** specializes in brassware and pottery; **Pekalongan** produces some of the finest batik in the country, much sought after by the Javanese élite.

Semarang thrives as a go-ahead port city often visited by cruise ships which use it as a base for excursions to the Dieng Plateau and the royal cities. Already wealthy in Dutch times, the old part of town contains a good scattering of buildings from the colonial period. The new residential area preens itself on a hill overlooking Tanjung Emas, the harbour. Chinese influence has always been strong, helping Semarang become a *jamu* (herbal remedy) centre. The "*jamu* lady" remains a familiar sight throughout Java. Dressed in a sarong, bag of homemade cures and pick-me-ups slung on her back, she dispenses her elixirs to ready buyers up and down the streets. Semarang's factories produce the packaged version for nationwide distribution in shops. Health enthusiasts and botanists enjoy the **Nyouya Meneer factory** where there's a museum on the subject and an herbarium of tropical medicinal plants.

Thay Kak Sie, a Chinese temple ornate with carved rafters, paintings and antiques, dates back to 1772. Another temple, **Sam Poo Kong**, on the road to Kendal west of Semarang, was named after an envoy of the Ming Dynasty who was influential in spreading Islamic beliefs. Built in the 15th century, it's sacred to Chinese and Muslim pilgrims alike.

The mosque at **Demak,** north-east of Semarang, is the oldest on Java and is a revered place of pilgrimage. **Kudus** has a picturesque old district spread around its 16th-century Al Manar Mosque. The delicately sculptured stone mausoleum nearby is the tomb of a holy man. Visit the town's *kretek* factory to see how they manufacture those heady, clove scented cigarettes—originally invented to cure chest complaints!

One of Indonesia's most original and talented women was born in **Mayong**, near Kudus, in 1879. Raden Ajeng Kartini, daughter of a Javanese aristocrat, the governor of Japara Regency, attended a Dutch school and became involved in national independence and women's

rights, which she expounded in letters to Dutch friends. She married a progressive Javanese official, the Regent of Rembang, and planned to open a school for Javanese girls. She died in 1904 after the birth of a son but her letters, published in 1911 under the title *Door duisternis tot licht* ("Through Darkness into Light") remain a classic. Kartini's birthday, 21 April, was made a national holiday. She is buried near **Jepara**, 35 km (22 miles) to the north, a town producing some of the best woodcarving in Java.

A good main highway south from Semarang gives access to the Dieng Plateau, continuing on to Yogyakarta. **Gedung Songo**, a 9th-century temple group dedicated to Shiva, is set on the slopes of Mt Ungaran, near Bandungan. It's worth the pretty strenuous climb for the ruins and unforgettable panoramic view over Lake Rawapening to Mt Merapi, Central Java's "Fire Mountain", smoking in the distance. Pause at little **Ambarawa** to visit the Railway Museum where grand old giants of the steam age are displayed in all their glory. A vintage locomotive sometimes makes the 15-km (9-mile) journey on the ancient cog railway from Jambu to Bedono; train-lovers can negotiate a trip with the station master at Ambarawa. **Magelang**, a crossroads town on the south road, has entered history as the place where Prince Diponegoro was taken prisoner by the Dutch in 1829.

Dieng

The more scenic route from Tasikmalaya through Central Java passes by Purwokerto. **Baturaden**, 14 km (9 miles) to the north, is an enchanting hill resort at the foot of Mt Slamet in an area brimming with springs and waterfalls—including a cascade pouring seven prongs of steaming water over sulphur-yellow rock formations. Heading coastward via Gombang, visit **Jatijajar**, the crown prince of caves, complete with life-size carved limestone figures. At **Karangbolong** ("Perforated Rock"), thousands of sea swallows camp down the sheer face of a cliff. Locals descend shaky bamboo ladders to pluck the nests, prized internationally for birds' nest soup.

The Prambanan temples are only part of the extraordinary architectural wealth of Java.

Basking in its role as gateway to the Dieng Plateau, peaceful little **Wonosobo** thrives as an affluent rural township. The road winds up from here to the "Home of the Gods", raised in honour of Shiva. The erstwhile holy city rests at more than 2,000 m (656 ft) in the damp, spongy caldera of an ancient volcano. Scarves of mist entwine you as you mount into the soft bluish greens and greys of terraced market gardens and stone walls.

The temples await, grouped on flat, marshy land. Built from the 9th century on by the Saliendra royal families, these Hindu-Buddhist sanctuaries are all that remain of an extensive complex once containing more than 200 temples and approached by stone steps known as Buddha's Stairway. They spent long years buried under vegetation, shaken periodically by earthquakes, to be rediscovered only last century, when local people crowned each surviving monument with a name drawn from the *Mahabharata.* Square and stocky, sparse in decorative elements, their timeless, simple beauty adds an unearthly quality to the mysterious setting. Even more so when Muslim prayer calls from the village below drift up, the newer faith solacing and encompassing the remnants of the old.

Posed together like mourning figures in a surrealist ballet are Sembadra, Puntadewa, Srikandi, Arjuna and Semar. Candi Gatotkaca stands aloof, to the south, and further south still is Candi Bima, the most haunting of all, with sculptured heads gazing over the plain. The plateau also carries remains of old palaces and monasteries. Many little caves are still used as places of religious retreat; they include Gua Semar, named for the great clown of Hindu mythology. A large stone near the entrance resembles the misshapen body of this favourite *wayang* character, whose rough jokes and inward nobility make him the beloved symbol of the common people.

Yogyakarta and Vicinity

The whole "special district" of Yogyakarta contains a population of about 3 million, with 500,000 living in the city itself—which still manages to seem like an overgrown village. Yogyakarta and nearby Surakarta (Solo) were created when the Second Mataram Empire divided in 1755 into two "self-ruling" sultanates with real political control in Dutch hands. In 1946 Yogyakarta was briefly capital of Indonesia, and revolutionary headquarters were established in the palace. In consequence, this was declared a Special Region, in direct contact with the central government without having to pass through the administrative channels of Central Java. In 1973 the liberal and charismatic Sultan Hamengkubuwono IX became vice-president of the Indonesian Republic.

Yogya isn't just another city. For Indonesians it's a place where religion, tradition and the most purely concentrated art forms mingle to create a unique atmosphere. It takes time to catch this courtly rhythm. You will sense a subtlety, a deeper meaning, trembling in the air like gong music. Yogyakarta, and especially the palace around which it revolves, is layers-deep in symbols.

Stroll along the lively main street, **Jl. Malioboro**, to get the feel of the city and pick up information at the Tourist Office. The graceful building standing amongst lawns and flowers was used by the Dutch Resident in colonial times, then as Sukarno's residence when Yogyakarta was briefly capital of the new republic. **Fort Vredeburg**, in front, was erected as a Dutch army headquarters.

Kraton Ngayogyakarta Hadiningrat, to give its full name, is the sultan's palace, to the south of Alun-alun Lor, the big square dominated by the Great Mosque. Visitors are required to wear suitably discreet clothing, for this is a holy spot as much as a palace. Passes can be obtained at the Tourist Office near the main entrance.

Construction of the palace, designed in classical Javanese style, began in 1775 under Sultan Hamangkubuwono I. Some 25,000 people, including members of the royal family, soldiers, guards and courtiers, live within the palace limits, a complex arrangement of courtyards, pavilions, batik and silver workshops, schools, markets and numerous other buildings. Number, form, colour and architectural details, even the type and positioning of the trees, have symbolic meaning. Chronograms—heraldic-looking combinations of real and mythological beasts—record dates in the Javanese calendar. A crown stands for 1, a leech represents 3, a dragon is 8, and so on. Hire a guide, who'll explain all these intricacies.

Giant stone figures stand guard at the gateway. Inside, two open-sided pavilions in the **Sri Manganti** courtyard contain antique gamelan ensembles used on ceremonial occasions, the Sultan's sedan chair in which he is carried to the mosque, and several wedding palanquins. **Bangsal Kencono**, the Golden Pavilion completed in 1792, is supported by gilded, carved teak columns and serves as coronation, wedding and reception hall. **Gedong Kuning** (Yellow House, 1756) is reserved for visits by the sultan and his family with, nearby, a repository for sacred heirlooms. An excellent **museum**, just renovated, houses antique lamps, china, lavish ceremonial costumes and fascinating old portraits and photographs of former sultans and their families. Outside, swallows swoop, twittering, through a thoroughly European little bandstand with Dutch stained-glass panels depicting musical instruments.

Regular classical dance rehearsals and gamelan performances are organized within the palace. You can obtain complete, up-to-date details from the Tourist Board or your hotel.

You may also be fortunate enough to witness one of the big Islamic festivals. Though the sultan is an enlightened modern politician, he still has a semi-magical power in the eyes of the people. His hair and nail clippings are kept. His religious role, typical of Java, is an Islamic interpretation of Hindu-Buddhist and animist practices. He still despatches annual gifts to the goddess of the South Sea and sends food and batik to placate his ominously powerful neighbours, the Lawu and Merapi volcanoes.

West of the palace stretches **Taman Sari**, the partially renovated "water palace" built in 1758 for the sultan by a Portuguese architect. It's a picturesque folly of pools and arcades. In the same neighbourhood is a small animal and bird market and many art and batik shops.

On Alun-alun Utara, the square north of the palace, the **Sonobudoyo Museum** displays superb objects including puppets, *wayang topek* masks, antique gamelan and a collection of krises.

Yogya boasts another charming, much smaller royal residence, **Pakualamen**, on Jl. Sultan Agung, along with a **museum** showing traditional weapons, musical instruments and ceremonial umbrellas (open Monday and Thursday only from 9 a.m. to 1 p.m.). In the prolongation of the same street, to the east, is the **Batik and Handicraft Research Centre**, offering free guided tours in the morning. If you'd like to learn how to do batik yourself, this is the best place to follow a course. Once you're an expert on the subject, venture into the bustling (and hustling!) market near the Tourist Information Centre, **Pasar Beringharjo**, where you might find an old second-hand batik, if you're lucky.

One of the country's most celebrated artists, **Affandi**, lived on Jl. Solo in the north-eastern part of the city; his daughter Kartika, herself an artist, displays a selection of their works in the adjacent gallery. Nearby is the **Saptohudoyo gallery** belonging to another artist and his wife, who together have assembled a collection of rare and beautiful objects from all the islands, displayed in a setting of princely tropical splendour.

There's an old royal cemetery in **Kotagede**, a quiet little town 6 km (4 miles) from Yogyakarta whose main reputation rests on its silver workshops. **Kasongan**, south-west, is a pottery village. **Imogiri** remains the official graveyard for the royal families of Yogyakarta and Solo. Visitors are allowed into some areas on Monday and Friday afternoon but must wear formal Javanese dress, which can be hired on the spot.

At **Parangtritis** the Indian Ocean breaks in silky green rollers and showers of creamy lace on a beach of inscrutable iron-grey sand. It's crowded with tourists at weekends but otherwise is a very pleasant, quiet place.

Directly west of Solo and north of Yogyakarta, **Mt Merapi** is one of the world's most restless volcanoes, but it can be climbed. The starting-point is the vulcanology station at Selo. It's a really tough haul, best undertaken at night to experience all the pyrotechnics—and only for the young and brave. Otherwise keep yourself in readiness for the Bromo trip (see page 66). If you do tackle Merapi, take warm gear.

Borobudur

Work on this gigantic temple, an hour's drive north-west of Yogya, was started around AD 800 by a monarch of the Sailendra dynasty employing thousands of local people. The building, a mass of grey andesite stone around a natural hillock, rises 31 m (101 ft) to the Great Stupa at the top. When Stamford Raffles saw it in 1815 it was completely overgrown. Some restoration work was done at the beginning of this century but the temple remained in a perilous condition until the Indonesian Government and UNESCO, aided by private donations, began the 10-year task of renovation, completed in 1983.

Each terrace represents a stage towards perfection in human life, and the principle is to climb from one terrace to the next, always keeping the reliefs on the right-hand side. The lower level of terraces represents *khamadhatu,* the world of desires, with a series of bas-reliefs depicting the transitory pleasures of worldly

existence. The next five galleries, marvellously carved with scenes from the life of Buddha, represent *rupadhatu,* the sphere of form. Three circular terraces with a number of miniature stupas in trellised stonework, each containing a seated Buddha, make a transition between the sphere of form and the final stage, *arupadhatu.* The last, overpoweringly large, plain stupa symbolizes *nirvana,* ultimate release and reality.

To appreciate Borobudur fully, see it at the Waicak Festival in May, when hundreds of people converge on the temple as the full moon appears on the horizon. And imagine how it must have looked eleven centuries ago, glowing with painted stucco, when the pilgrims saw it as a great, spiked crown on the dark earth, responding with flashes of jewel colour to the flickering of their lamps.

The May pilgrimage begins at **Candi Mendut**, a smaller temple 3 km (almost 2 miles) to the east. It contains carved panels and three powerful stone statues in an interior pierced with a shaft so that sun or moonlight can fall on the huge, central, seated Buddha.

Prambanan

The Hindu complex at Prambanan, 17 km (10½ miles) north-east of Yogya, was completed in about 900. Restoration is almost complete on the temples to Brahma, Shiva and Vishnu, while several minor

buildings are in a state of ruin. The golden stone of the largest temple, dedicated to Shiva the Destroyer, is carved with a multitude of sweet-faced human and superhuman beings, animals, birds, leaves and fruit in tales from the *Ramayana*. If Borobudur impressed or even oppressed you with its size and spiritual austerity, then Prambanan will enchant with its frolicsome human qualities. If you're there at the right time, don't miss a performance of the Ramayana ballet, held four nights each month from May to October when the moon is full.

There are many other Hindu-Buddhist monuments in the area. Take the road behind the Prambanan complex to **Candi Sewu** and **Candi Plaoson**, approached across a landscape of silk-cotton trees and sugarcane. **Candi Sari** stands in vegetation, a textured world of young rice, papaya and jackfruit trees. Close to the main Yogya–Solo road, **Candi Kalasan** houses a bat colony and a beautiful carved *kala* (demon) head. **Ratu Boko**, an old fortress monastery, involves a short, steep climb and is worth visiting as much for the panorama as the ruins.

Surakarta

This city, usually known as Solo, is actually bigger than Yogyakarta, with an urban population of more

From the heights of Borobudur he has bestowed his serene smile on more than a thousand years.

than 500,000. Whereas Yogyakarta espoused Independence, Solo's leading families retained strong ties with the Dutch whose protection permitted a tremendous flowering of art and culture. Consequently, although the sultan of Yogya holds certain hereditary authority, the Solo royal family was divested of its power.

Located on the Solo River, the town is reputed for the restrained indigos, cream and brown of its batik, its gamelan, *wayang kulit*, dance and meditation centres. The Tourist Office is on the main street, Jl. Slamet Riyadi, next door to the **Radyapustaka Museum**, which displays Javanese crafts, a collection of krises and mementos of the royal family.

South of the main street, **Kraton Hadiningrat**, the larger of Solo's two palaces, was swept by fire in 1985. It has since been restored, but some of the original (1745) parts remain, built in the Javanese "umbrella" style. Also saved was the watchtower where the sultan traditionally meditates before his mystic meeting with the goddess of the South Sea (see p.49); dances associated with the event take place in the courtyard below. The big audience pavilion, encrusted with Venetian glass, is used for ceremonies four times a year as well as for weddings and circumcisions, when nine princesses dance in the gracious, composed Solo style.

Seven side doors, symbolic of Hindu-Buddhist progress to the

57

"seventh heaven", mark the way from the main gate to the sultan's private apartments. Hindu objects, coronation chairs, 200-year-old ceremonial umbrellas and antique krises are displayed in the **museum**, along with some splendid 18th-century royal carriages—which, in the heyday of the sultanate, were drawn by fastidiously groomed white bulls.

Mangkunegaran Palace is located north of Jl. Slamet Riyadi. Completed in 1866, it's the seat of a subsidiary branch of the Solo royal family and has the sun as its symbol. Drowsy sunlight and serene tropical gardens bright with singing birds add to the magical atmosphere of a place where time seems to have stood still. The present prince is a businessman with an intense interest in the arts and a relaxed approach to opening areas of his private apartments to visitors. Excellent guides lead you to the audience pavilion, a supreme example of Javanese architecture in solid teak enhanced by Dutch lamps, with a raised platform at the end for *wayang kulit*.

Among the extraordinary jewellery, coins, lamps and krises in the palace **museum** (including krises traditionally worn by women in their hair), note the chastity belts—for men as well as women. The palace also contains two 200-year-old gamelan orchestras named "Drifting in Smiles" and "Reign of Love", as well as impeccably maintained royal carriages, still used on special occasions. Batik is made and sold on the premises and a *wayang berber* artist is present on Mondays to explain this ancient form of *wayang*, a little like early cinema. Cultural performances and palace dinners are available by arrangement.

The Sound of Moonlight

Once upon a time, a god, Sang Hyang Guru, ruled all of Java from his mountain palace. Calling the lesser immortals together proved difficult—so he made three gongs, each tuned to a different pitch. This is said to be the origin of gamelan ("hammer"). In time, two kinds of music developed: "loud" for grand occasions; "soft" for intimate moments. Eventually, in the 17th century, they combined.

The gamelan orchestra is made up of about 20 instruments, almost all percussion—the gongs themselves, types of kettledrums, cymbals and xylophones, plus flutes and strings. The oldest examples, said to date from the 12th century, can be seen in the palaces of Yogyakarta and Solo. There are two musical scales: pelog, the 7-tone system and slendro, 5 tones, said to be older. The music is reflective, directed at achieving total peace for the performers and the listener. Jaap Kuunst, an authority on Indonesian music, captured its essence for all time when he wrote: "Gamelan ... is pure and mysterious like moonlight and always changing like flowing water... it is a state of being, such as moonlight itself which lies poured out over the land."

58

Curio-buyers adore **Pasar Triwundu**, the fleamarket, where you'll find some real bargains if you hunt around. **Pasar Klewer** is a huge fabric market with a mind-boggling choice of batik. And you can plunge back into the delights of childhood with a visit to the **toy market**, held in front of Radyapustaka Museum (the best day is Sunday).

Sangiran

The fossilized cranium of *Pithecanthropus erectus* was found by a Dutch professor at Sangiran, 15 km (9 miles) north of Solo, in 1936, setting the compass for scholarly surmises about the existence of human life in this place some 250,000 years ago. There's a tiny modern **museum** where you're likely to be the only visitor eyeing the gigantic tusks of extinct species of elephant, bones of apes, crocodiles, rhinoceros and deer, models of skulls, and a startling diorama dramatizing distant ancestors at work and play. Villagers crowd the entrance offering fossils, the fake and the true, along with stone adzes and axes (some just chipped into shape yesterday) and semi-precious stones. Someone's sure to lead you up to a ridge to look out at the spot where the famous remains were found.

Candi Sukuh

On the slopes of Mt Lawu, 36 km (22 miles) east of Solo, up an extremely difficult and winding road (4-wheel drive vehicle recommended), Sukuh Temple commands one of the most fantastic views anywhere in the world. Down below, minutely terraced hillsides planted with tea; in the distance, the shimmering Solo River; all around a sweep of sky, hills and rolling forest breathtaking in its majesty. The Hindu-Buddhist temple was built here, at 1,000 m (3,280 ft), at the close of the 15th century, a date bearing no relation to the achievement itself, for Sukuh's spiritual ancestry seems to lie with the stepped pyramids of Latin America or the those of Egypt. It is sacred to Bima, a warrior in the *Mahabharata* epic. The bas-reliefs and phallic carvings in rough, blackish stone express power and virility rather than the eroticism often claimed for them. Strange flat stones in the shape of turtles serve as steps for the main structure. This mysterious place is possessed by some unfathomable magic. Locals claim that it was a women's temple and that its counterpart, **Candi Ceto** on the nearby peak, was for men. A series of 15th-century thatched pavilions built on terraces up a steep slope, Candi Ceto is nothing compared to its secretive and darkly compelling neighbour.

EAST JAVA

Giant turtles, tigers, temples, bull-races and a beautiful landscape culminating in rumbling Mt Bromo— these are some of the draws of East Java. It's also Indonesia's most industrialized province; the capital, Surabaya, is the country's second largest city.

The generations intent on building Borobudur ignored the claims of war and commerce, and in the 10th century Central Java's power declined and the emphasis shifted here. A philosopher-king, Airlangga, ascended the throne in 1019. During his prosperous reign many temples were built, and parts of the *Mahabharata* were translated and reinterpreted according to local belief. At his death, rivalry divided the region until the Kediri brought it under control for some 200 years. Later, Singosari rule, although brief and violent (1222–92) bequeathed a further treasury of temple architecture along with the Shiva-Buddhist faith. The Majapahit dynasty took over at the end of the 15th century, establishing an empire stretching as far as the Malay peninsula and the Philippines before falling to the assault of northern Islamic groups dominated, in turn, by late Mataram rulers from Central Java.

Around Blitar

Just outside **Blitar**, an impressive monument honours the burial place of Sukarno, Indonesia's first president. Known as *Makam Proklamator* ("Grave of the Proclaimer of Independence"), it was built in 1978, eight years after his death, over the previously unmarked grave in the little war cemetery. Removed from real power after suspected involvement in the attempted Communist takeover of 1965, the national leader can now again safely be recognized as the "Father of Indonesia", a reinstated charismatic figure for the crowds who come to pay homage.

The superb Hindu temple complex at **Panataran**, 11 km (7 miles) north of Blitar, was begun in about 1197 by Singosari kings, took 250 long years to build and was finally completed under Majapahit rule. It's the biggest sanctuary in East Java and one of the largest in the country. The main gateway leads to the Dated Temple (the inscription 1292 over the entrance corresponds to AD 1369 in the western calendar). On a higher level, Naga Temple is named for its sinuous procession of huge carved snakes, placed there as a warning to shady characters who might have ideas about making off with the sacred treasures. The base of the main temple carries depictions of Hanuman, the monkey god, and his loyal army, enacting part of the story related in the *Ramayana*. Crocodiles, bulls, tortoises and flowers are carved around the little 15th-century bathing place.

South-west of Blitar at **Ngliyep**, the goddess of the South Sea is up to her old tricks, pounding away at the coast, exacting protracted ceremonies and annual offerings. She's better behaved at **Pacitan**, where there are beautiful swimming places right near the provincial boundary with Central Java and a "musical cave"—the astounding gamelan effects are achieved by striking the stalactites with stones.

Malang and Vicinity

This delightful little town on the Brantas River is one of the province's main hill resorts. Founded by the Dutch in the 18th century, graced with avenues of shady trees, airy parks and old colonial buildings, it makes an ideal base for the area. From there, in a series of day trips, you can visit the Singosari temples; the Majapahit sanctuaries near Blitar can also be seen on a one-day outing. Mt Bromo, the biggest tourist draw in the whole of East Java, is easily accessible from Malang. You could then spend the night at Tosari before proceeding to Surabaya, from where there's an easy ferry trip to Madura.

Start with **Candi Singosari**, 10 km (6 miles) to the north. This unfinished temple was erected about the time of the assassination of Kertanegara, the bloodthirsty monarch whose statue now stands in Surabaya. Near the temple are two monstrous giants, guardians of the gateway to the Singosari capital.

To the east of Malang, **Candi Jago** dates back to 1268. It's the presumed resting place of the fourth king of Singosari, possessing carved scenes from the *Mahabharata* in flat, *wayang kulit* style. The slender sanctuary nearby, **Candi Kidal**, was completed in 1260 to honour another Singosari monarch; it stands as a recognized gem of East Javanese temple art. Carved garudas guard the building decorated with vigorous *kala* heads to turn away evil.

At **Lawang**, 18 km (11^1/$_2$ miles) north of Malang, locals claim that Hotel Niagara is haunted by the ghosts of three women. Certainly this five-storey Art Nouveau palace, designed for a Chinese timber exporter by a Brazilian architect, offers ideal accommodation for spectral visitors who should feel perfectly at home descending the once magnificent staircase to glide across terrazzo floors, surrounded by stained glass, painted tiles and languorous flower motifs. Shake off the other world with a walk in **Kebun Raya Purwodadi** botanical gardens further north, specializing in high altitude dry-climate plants including several rare species of cacti, palms and orchids. Another branch of the Bogor Gardens, it covers 85 ha (210 acres).

Batu, 15 km (9 miles) north-west of Malang, is known for its apples. Baskets of them fill the markets in season, along with citrus fruits, tomatoes, and delicious melons. **Songgoriti** and flowery **Selecta** are attractive villages on the slopes of Mt Arjuna; to the north is **Sumber Brantas**, the source of the Brantas River.

Overleaf: Dawn mists roll apart to reveal the ancient caldera known as the Sand Sea.

Surabaya and Vicinity

The provincial capital is said to have sprung up on the site of a tussle between a shark, *sura,* and a crocodile, *buaya.* Surabaya, with its population of some 3¾ milllion, second largest city in Indonesia, doesn't claim to be beautiful, but it can claim to be brave. Indonesians call it the City of Heroes. When the Japanese surrendered in 1945, Lord Louis Mountbatten, head of the Allies' South-East Asia command, sent in British troops to oversee the peace process. The Indonesians interpreted it as a manoeuvre to hand the country back to the Dutch, and fighting broke out. Surabaya was bombarded for three days and nights. Although the British won, the Indonesians themselves were astonished by the city's extraordinary courage—and so were the Dutch. The Battle of Surabaya drew world attention and eventually proved crucial in gaining independence for the whole country.

It's a major harbour and commercial town, not the sort of place you'd choose for a holiday but still retaining some of its "Surabaya Johnny" atmosphere in the tougher districts.

For a glimpse of its sea-going past, visit the wharves at **Kalimas**. You might have to pay a very small fee and you won't be allowed to photograph, but you'll have a close-up of rakish sailing ships and be able to capture a little lost atmosphere from the time when Surabaya was

synonymous with dangerous days and roistering, hell-bent nights.

The **Heroes' Monument** is a plain, white, rocket-shaped column on Jl. Pahlawan. It commemorates Indonesians who died in the freedom struggle.

Jl. Tunjungan, in the centre of town, is one of the best shopping streets in Indonesia, rivalling Singapore for inexpensive electronic goods and cameras. There's nostalgia in the **Majapahit Hotel** in the same street. It was *the* place for fashionable gatherings in Dutch times. Some of its grandeur remains in the fine staircase and an interior tropical garden filled with statues. The Indonesian flag was raised first on this hotel during the Battle of Surabaya and the statue outside represents the Spirit of Nationalism.

The residence of the Governor of East Java on Jl. Pemuda was originally a Dutch mansion. Across the road, a very old **Buddhist monument** honours Kertanegara, last ruler of the Javanese kingdom of Singosari. Its impressive title is *Joko Dolog* ("Guardian of Young Teak") but locals spoil the effect by calling it "the fat boy". The king was no saint. When the Emperor of China sent envoys, he cut off their noses and tattooed "No!" on their foreheads before returning them home. He was finally murdered in his own palace but his memorial, quite illogically, has a reputation for curing illnesses. A few coins or flowers at the foot seem to do the trick.

The **zoo** is the finest in the country. If you don't feel like walking you can be pedalled around in style in a *becak* to visit a marvellous collection of birds, animals, fish and reptiles and an excellent nocturnal house. The world's largest lizard, the Komodo dragon, is reared in this zoo, and the ugly specimens on view constitute its biggest attraction by far. There's a well-maintained **museum** opposite the zoo entrance.

Commerce hasn't entirely excluded culture in Surabaya, and two famous East Javanese dances are regularly performed here. *Reog Ponorogo* represents a fight between Javanese aristocrats and an army of tigers and peacocks. The main dancer wears a tiger mask topped by a tremendous fan of peacock feathers and keeps it all in place by holding a strap between his teeth. *Kuda Kepang*, the "horse trance dance" is often staged at the same time; it involves "riding" a plaited bamboo horse. At the height of the action, performers enter a trance and eat glass—lightbulbs are particularly relished. Inquire at your hotel or at the East Java Promotion Board for details of time and place. A special performance can be arranged if you give enough notice.

On Jl. Kusumabangsa there's an amusement park, **Taman Hiburan Rakyat**, staging *wayang, ludruk* (Javanese comedy) along with other theatrical events. It's also a good place for shopping, open from 7 p.m. till midnight.

The remains of the first Islamic settlement on Java can be seen at **Gresik**, 25 km (15$^{1}/_{2}$ miles) to the west of Surabaya. The Arab quarter is decidedly picturesque, and the town boasts Java's oldest Muslim gravestone, dated 1419. **Trowulan**, south-west, used to be capital of the Majapahit Empire. Remains are scattered over a large area and there is a good museum displaying terracotta figurines. There's a good map there pinpointing other spots of historic interest. The excellent museum at **Mojokerto**, 42 km (27 miles) south-west of Surabaya, has an exhibition of Majapahit carving and a magnificent 11th-century relief of Vishnu mounted on a garuda.

Directly south of Surabaya, **Pandaan**, an agreeable hill resort, reposes beneath Mt Penanggungan. Ballet is performed in **Taman Candrawilwatikta** amphitheatre, including an East Javan version of the *Ramayana*.

Volcanoes and Nature Reserves

Long ago, a powerful giant kept his beautiful daughter away from harm deep within his mountain fastness. She eventually made her way to the outer world, where everything enchanted her—but nothing so much as a handsome youth, the first man, apart from her father, she had ever met. He was the son of Bromo, another mountain giant, and the two fathers were sworn enemies. She threatened to throw herself into

Bromo's fiery crater if she couldn't have her way, so her father set her lover an impossible task: he was to dig a sea of sand around Bromo between sunset and sunrise, and if he succeeded, the couple could marry. Using a *batok* (coconut-shell cup), he set to work at sundown, but before dawn the jealous father crowed like a cock, inciting all the village birds to follow suit. Thinking dawn had broken, the prince flung his scoop away in despair; it turned into Mt Batok. He had time only to cry *Kembang Manis* ("Sweet Flower") to his lost bride before dawn really did break, and both were turned to stone. Heartbroken, Bromo still grieves his daughter, heaving sighs of smoke into the sky. Peace will come to him when the lovers are finally united.

The Tenggerese believe their ancestors are buried on Widodaren ("Bride"), one of the mountains in the ancient crater referred to as the Sand Sea. Batok is now extinct; **Bromo** itself overpowers them both, filling the sky as you approach. Slowly dying but still forceful, it has spilled rich lava over the land, and chastized neglect with fire and molten rock.

When Java was converted to Islam, high-ranking families took refuge on Bali but many of the others withdrew to these remote hills where they practise combined Buddhism and Hinduism incorporating older beliefs. Some 300,000 Tenggerese people live in about 40 villages in the Bromo area. Thanks to Bromo's largesse, they cultivate marvellous vegetable gardens. They honour their god of fire on the Buddah's birthday, winding across the whispering Sand Sea, torches flaring, then run barefoot into the crater towards the jets of steam 200 m (656 ft) below with offerings of flowers, chickens and vegetables.

Whether your main base is Malang or Surabaya, it's advisable to halt overnight near Bromo, either at one of the westerly approach villages (Sukapura, Ngadisari, Cemoro Lawang) or at Tosari, on the easterly route. If you're determinedly athletic, you could trek in via Ngadas to the south, but seek local advice first. Road transport from both Ngadisari and Tosari will take you to within walking or horse-riding distance from Bromo. Wear warm clothing, including jacket and gloves: temperatures can drop to zero.

The classic approach is to leave Surabaya by jeep about midnight, arriving at Ngadisari around two in the morning when the air is cold and sweet with the scent of pine; blanketed Tenggerese huddle around

Mount Batak fills the sky as Tenggerese mountain people lead you to Bromo, the holy volcano.

charcoal fires in the village street. Among them you'll find a guide and a small, neat-footed horse to ride into the dark along precipitous paths. At Cemoro Lawang, you stop at a sleepy inn for hot ginger drinks; then you're crossing the Sand Sea, dust the colour of anthracite scuffing beneath the horse's hooves. You'll stare into Bromo's orange eye before dawn, then see the sun mount out of Bali, illuminating the unreal landscape for the return ride.

Taking the alternative route through Tosari, many visitors prefer to sleep a few hours there, then take road transport to view the sunrise from Penanjakan, continuing by jeep almost to the foot of the volcano. Whichever route you choose, you'll have to scale a concrete staircase of 250 steps to enter the world of sulphurous fumes and accompanying rumbles.

The eastern end of Java is dominated by the six volcanic peaks of the **Ijen Plateau**, one of the principal sources of sulphur for the chemicals industry. It's rough going to visit **Kawah Ijen**, a turquoise crater lake streaked with sulphur enclosed in walls of sheer white rock. This area is more reputed for its weird landscape than for animal life.

The **Meru Betiri Reserve** on the south-east coast claims to be the last haunt of Java's tigers. There are fewer than half-a-dozen left, including a large male. Though footprints are sometimes found, the animals keep out of sight. Civets, leopards, jungle cats and monkeys are slightly more gregarious.

Conservation efforts are concentrated on the turtles at Sukamade

---

The Kris

An object of magic and ritual, the kris is prayed over, ritually cleansed with oil of sandalwood, honoured with incense and offerings and kept swathed in silken cloth. Although a weapon, it is also symbolic of its owner's very being, while having a life of its own. The Madurese used to increase its strength by rubbing it with snake entrails and scorpion blood.

The art of damascening was introduced by Persian smiths in the 13th century and developed by the Indonesian empus (kris-makers). In this technique, pamor, a nickeliferous meteoritic iron, is beaten onto the blade, itself forged from a darker iron. The blade could be straight, curved or wavy, with an uneven number of luk (curves). The finest krises were made during the Majapahit period (1293–1478). An extraordinary carved relief at Sukuh Temple shows Bima, a Hindu warrior and metal-working god, beating out a kris on an anvil while his brother, Arjuna, works the bellows.

Today the true art of sacred kris-making has been lost and the object is purely ceremonial, worn on special occasions and otherwise treasured as a family heirloom. But belief in its spiritual potency remains unquestioned.

Beach. On moonlit nights they come ashore to lay their eggs. Travel in this region is difficult.

Baluran National Park, on the other hand, is easily accessible and you can get around quite easily in a 4-wheel-drive vehicle. Conditions for game-watching here are unique, for part of the area is savannah, and in the dry season when rivers are parched, animals gather at the watering-holes—a touch of Africa. You'll see *banteng*, wild pig, leopards, monitor lizards, monkeys and a cross-section of bird life. Banyuwangi is only an hour away, and from there the boats cross to Bali.

Madu

A fairly big island only 30 minutes from Surabaya by passenger or car ferry, Madura claims fame for its hot-tempered, sea-going men, dark, pretty women and its extraordinary, fleet-footed bulls. Bull races, kerapan sapi, take place regularly between August and October; they can also be specially arranged for tourist groups. The newest stadium is at Bangkalan, about 16 km (10 miles) inland from the Kamal boat terminal.

They're heroic looking creatures, these bulls. Their coats gleam like bronze and their polished horns are crowned with tassels and ribbon. The Madurese groom them, massage them, talk to them, feed them on a diet which includes honey, beer, tots of rum and up to 50 raw eggs a day, and even sing them to sleep.

It all began when ploughmen raced their bulls down a ricefield. Nowadays, two animals are harnessed together and the "jockey" lies spread on a skeleton chariot between them, shouting, clinging, urging, as the slender hooves pound to the finishing-line. Only two pairs are raced at a time, so it takes several elimination heats to find the winners. Before the race, gamelan music is played to pep them up. Afterwards, there's more gamelan to calm them down. Cattle are the island's wealth and pride and local government prizes are offered at major meetings to encourage stock breeding.

The two that get their legs over the line carry the day. Gentle as the creatures are, they run blind and often veer off into the crowd—so stay put in the grandstand. There's a tiny museum right by the bull stadium.

Madura isn't a rich island, the soil is poor and much of the livelihood comes from fishing and salt. Still, you'll glimpse some pretty scenes: women in curious pointed hats cutting rice very slowly, a few stalks at a time so as not to frighten the rice goddess; rickety carts pulled by oxen who didn't make it into the big time; a beautiful old Muslim cemetery at **Air Mata** (inland from Arosbaya); brown-sailed fishing boats at south-coast villages near Tanjung. In this area the batik is exceptional because natural dyes are used, obtained from moss and bark. You can buy it on the spot or in Surabaya.

BALI

Heaven, the Balinese tell you, is exactly like Bali. It must be one of the loveliest places on earth. Within a golden rim of beaches, an irregular landscape of deep ravines, fast-flowing rivers and paddy fields rises gently in curved tiers up to a volcanic chain, culminating in Mt Agung at the island's eastern end. The gods live there, close (a little too close for comfort) to the Balinese who spend a great part of each day worshipping, pacifying and entertaining them.

Time is meaningless to the 3 million Balinese. They live to a rhythm of religious observance, work, rest and artistic creation which ends in death—followed by rebirth. On any day at any time you may run across a festival. No distinction is made between art and life, in fact there is no word for "art" or "artist" in the Balinese language. Women make exquisite offerings of folded palm-leaves, carvers turn out figure after figure, weavers work for weeks to create a length of material;

metalsmiths are considered aristocrats for their skill in producing musical instruments, religious accessories, farm implements and, in the past, the semi-magical krıs. Much of Balinese art, notably the vast, scintillating cremation decorations, is transitory.

The course of Bali's history was altered by the growth of Islam in Java which sent Hindu nobles, priests and artists in search of another island where their culture could survive. On Bali they blended with the local people, incorporating animist elements into the religion which developed into Hindu-Dharma. A fusion of Hinduism, Buddhism and ancestor worship, it governs every stage of life, from birth through the teeth-filing ceremony of adolescence and the ritual abduction before marriage, to joyful cremation ceremonies. For the Balinese, the world has to be balanced between the forces of good and evil, equally powerful, ceaselessly active; these adverse principles are symbolized by the black and white checked sarong swathed around statues.

Each *desa,* or village, is a tightly knit social group made up of a number of smaller units, *banjar.* Irrigation, planting, harvesting and threshing are community endeavours. Anyone wanting to live and work in

Life is a constant tussle between good and evil for the Balinese, who express it in dance.

another district has to ask permission from his *desa* and must contribute financially to make up for his absence. Solitude is unnatural as well as dangerous a prime opportunity for being captured by the ever-present spirits.

The island has been changed by tourism, and the islanders' commercial sense is increasing. Yet villagers still trek to southern beaches to stare in disbelief at the hotels and scantily clad visitors. Head inland to catch the magic—chances are you'll surrender completely to the spell of this "paradise on earth".

DENPASAR AND THE SOUTH

Tourist development has affected mainly the southern part of the island. A multitude of hotels, boutiques and restaurants has mushroomed where once there was nothing but a handful of small fishing villages. It's no use lamenting those long-departed days when this was a secret holiday hideaway; now it's up to its coconut fronds in providing sun, sea, sand, souvenirs, discos and fast food—and it can be very enjoyable. A few tiny, inexpensive eating-places still survive, but this isn't the real Bali, just a good base for fun and relaxation.

Denpasar

Though it's noisy and rather frazzling, you'll probably find yourself in the capital to make use of the facilities. Shops, banks and restaurants are centred on **Jl. Gajah Mada**. Try to make a morning trip to **Pasar Badung**, the odiferous, colourful main market, to take in the friendly atmosphere.

At one corner of busy **Alun-alun Puputan** is a large statue of a four-faced Hindu god, **Catur Muka**, blessing each direction. The Balinese believe it to be more effective than traffic lights, but they've got this one wrong, as you'll soon realize from the number of accidents on the chaotic roads. *Puputan* means "mass suicide", an old tradition in Bali where the people would rather die than be conquered, and the square commemorates a tragic event in Balinese history. In 1906 Dutch troops marched on Denpasar after a dispute between the rajas and the Dutch administration. As the militia surrounded the palace, the gates were thrown open and out poured the nobility and priests in ceremonial dress, leading their people bedecked in all their finery. A priest stabbed the raja through the heart: the signal for the other nobles to kill each other and their children, or throw themselves upon the Dutch weapons. The Dutch went on to vanquish the other resisting rajadoms in much the same inglorious way.

Various styles of palace and temple architecture coexist in **Museum Bali**, one of the largest museums in Indonesia, inaugurated by the Dutch in 1932 and displaying ancient stone implements, masks, woodcarvings and other artefacts from prehistoric to modern times. Don't miss the jewelled, 15th-century krises. **Pura Jagatnata**, the temple alongside in white coral, is dedicated to Sanghyang Widi, the Supreme God, represented by a golden statue. **St Joseph's Catholic Church** on Jl. Kepundung is thatched with palm fibre; six stone angels pose above the door in Balinese stances.

The **Arts Centre** on Jl. Nusa Indah at Abiankapas provides an area for performances and exhibitions. There's a festival in June and July; at other times, if you visit Kokar, the Conservatory of Performing Arts, you'll probably see young students rehearsing dances to the music of a gamelan ensemble.

Resorts

The young hang out at **Kuta**, north of the airport, where it's all happening. Kuta's lovely stretch of white sand, almost empty in the sixties, now swarms with swimmers and surfers, hawkers and hustlers, moneychangers and masseuses. The development is extending to Legian, further north, and threatening to swallow up Seminyak, too. Take heed of the danger signs on the beach if you swim or surf: the undertow can be treacherous.

Sanur, on the east coast, has a grander, staider reputation, though it also gets very crowded. Visit **Le Mayeur Museum**, a 2-minute stroll along the beach north from fashionable Bali Beach Hotel. The Belgian painter A.S. Le Mayeur built the cottage himself in 1932, surrounding it with lovely gardens bright with bougainvillaea and enhanced by statues and ponds. He lived there with his young Balinese wife, a famous *legong* dancer, and after his death she maintained it as a museum. Kite-flying is a favourite pastime of the local inhabitants; an annual contest is held in August when the trade winds are at their fiercest. The coastline here is completely enclosed by reef; you can hire a boat to visit it then set out on foot at low tide to nearby **Serangan**, "Turtle Island", to watch the turtles trundling in. Beautiful seashells can be found here, but beware of souvenirs of turtle shell; you will not be allowed to import them into your home country.

Nusa Dua is chic and manicured, an up-market resort where there's nothing much but sea, sun and sport. The "two islands" of the resort's name refer to two knobs of land each connected to the mainland of the Bukit peninsula by a narrow isthmus. North is Benoa, an uninteresting fishing village; at **Benoa Port** across the bay, cruise ships and yachts anchor.

On the south-west tip of the Bukit peninsula stands, or rather, hangs, **Uluwatu**. One of the island's holiest temples, it was built on the cliffside in the 10th century in grey volcanic stone, which the setting sun robes in glorious colour. **Suluban** beach, a few kilometres north, attracts devotees of surfing from everywhere, especially Australians.

THE EAST

Most of Bali's settlements are clustered in the eastern half of the island, dominated by the volcano Gunung Agung; the west is mainly mountainous and preserved as West Bali National Park. You can use the southern beaches as a base and visit the rest of the island as day trips, or stay in Ubud and branch out from there—it's an enchanting spot and the island's cultural centre, somehow managing to take tourism in its relaxed stride.

Ubud and Vicinity

Ubud and the little villages around it have always been famed for their painters and sculptors. The town's graceful way of life and natural beauty attracted art celebrities from all over the world, among them Walter Spies and Rudolph Bonnet who settled there in the thirties. They taught the Balinese the basics of Western techniques and greatly influenced local styles. Many foreign artists still live and work here; be sure of visiting the **galleries** of Antonio Blanco, an eccentric Catalan, and Dutchman Han Snel, who has also set up a restaurant and hotel. Bonnet helped create **Museum Puri Lukisan**, a gallery showing some of the best examples of modern Balinese painting and sculpture. You'll find it near the centre of Ubud, not far from the Tourist Office, a series of pavilions in a tropical garden. **Museum Neka**,

2 km (a good mile) outside the town beyond Campuan, has an excellent display of paintings by Indonesian and foreign artists, including Spies, Bonnet and Dutchman Ari Smidt who inspired the "Young Artists" school.

Near the Campuan bridge, **Pura Gunung Labah** is one of the most ancient temples on Bali, said to date from the 8th century. Shrouded in greenery, it overlooks **Goa Raksasa**, a cave named after the demonic giant who once dwelt there.

At the end of **Monkey Forest Road**, where a tribe of grey monkeys delight in pestering tourists for food and making off with anything they can grab, you'll come to **Pura Dalem**, a moss-grown temple with wonderfully expressive carvings.

On the southern outskirts of Ubud, **Peliatan** is reputed for its dance, gamelan, painting and carving. It's a good place to study *legong* dance; the troupe from here was the first Balinese company to perform abroad and starred with Bob Hope in the fifties in *The Road to Bali*. Visit the **Agung Rai Gallery** for an overview of the development of modern Balinese painting. **Pengosekan**, just to the south, is another artists' colony. The surrounding scenery is superb, perfect for walks.

Some of the most famous Balinese woodcarvers and maskmakers live in **Mas**, and the back streets are crowded with workshops. You'll find works of exceptionally

A temple door in Bali.
Art to honour the gods or for the sheer joy of living and creating?

high quality—at high prices—among a proliferation of less imaginative items. **Celuk**, closer to Denpasar, is devoted to silver- and goldsmiths noted for their filigree work and is very popular with tour buses. You can watch manufacturing techniques; prices are generally fixed. Make a turn-off for **Sukawati**, in the wind-chime business, or continue south to **Batubulan**, which proposes objects carved from soft sandstone. The road is lined with noble heroes and villainous demons—

pop-eyed and long-toothed. **Pura Puseh**, a temple close to the main highway, has some particularly fine examples of local stone-carving.

Mengwi is west of Ubud but easier reached from Denpasar if you have to depend on public transport. Its beautiful temple, **Pura Taman**

Ayun, stands serene within a double moat. It was built in 1634 and renovated in 1937; the stone gate and some of the shrine doors are beautifully carved. Continue from here north-east to **Sangeh Monkey Forest**. The trees are nutmegs, not indigenous to Bali, and said to have been part of a mountain carried by the flying monkey Hanuman that dropped off and fell to earth with its tribe of sprite monkeys. You can buy peanuts or fruit and spend hours watching the antics of whole families swinging from tree to tree and swarming over the lichen-covered forest temple, **Bukit Sari**. Hide your sunglasses, film, hats and other small items—they'll make off with anything poking out of your pockets. And don't provoke them: a monkey bite can be dangerous.

Petulu, 6 km (4 miles) north of Ubud, is best visited towards sunset when white herons zoom in to settle on the trees.

The road to Tampaksiring turns north at **Pejeng**; make a halt there to visit the archaeological museum and the temples. **Pura Kebo Edan** has a statue of Bima fighting a buffalo, hence the nickname "Crazy Buffalo Temple". **Pura Pusering Jagat**, the "Temple of the Navel of the World", dates from the 14th century and is a place of pilgrimage at full moon. In **Pura Penataran Sasih**, a huge solid bronze drum swings high up in the pavilion. Known as the Moon Drum, it is supposed to have fallen from the sky. It's carved in the style of a Bronze Age dynasty of Vietnam of around 300 BC.

Legend recounts that the god Indra created the holy spring of **Tirta Empul** near Tampaksiring by piercing the ground. Out gushed *amerta*, the water of immortality, which revived his ailing army. It is still believed to have healing powers, and throngs of people from all over Bali visit the pools for ritual purification. You'll need a temple scarf, which can be hired on the spot. Despite the hordes of vendors lining the pathway, the temple is a lovely place, with lily ponds and springs spouting from mossy walls. An inscription on a stone found nearby dates Tirta Empul to AD 962. Overlooking the temple is a resthouse built by the Dutch and transformed into a palace for Sukarno: it's said he installed a telescope on his balcony to watch the Balinese beauties bathing in the pools down below.

At **Gunung Kawi**, 1^1/$_2$ km (1 mile) from Tampaksiring, two rows of hollows are carved out of the rock face on opposite sides of a ravine. These 11th-century memorials commemorate a royal dynasty; a legendary giant scooped them out with his fingernails in a single night. The head of the same giant, Kebo Iwa, is portrayed in stone at Pura Gadun, a temple at **Blahbatuh** on the main

Tens of thousands of temples, and a life dominated by constant prayers and offerings.

Denpasar–Gianyar road. Reach it by turning south at Pejeng (see p. 76).

Excavation has revealed a large bathing pool dating from the 11th century at **Goa Gajah**, the Elephant Cave, near **Bedulu**. The fountains in the shape of seven nymphs represent the seven rivers of India. Inside the main cave, protected by huge demon face, are T-shaped niches which probably served as meditation chambers. The monks who lived here may have been Hindu, Buddhist or a combination of both, since the carvings show elements of each religion. A fairly steep scramble down the bank behind the pool leads to another cave with two ancient Buddha statues.

Gianyar is a good place to buy a sarong—you can watch the weavers at work in the back rooms of shops. There's an old palace in the centre of town but it's closed to the public; you'll have to make do with peering through the gates unless you have special permission to visit. **Bona**, to the south, is a basketry centre and home of the *kecak* dance. Sidan, 3 km (2 miles) east of Gianyar, is noted for the stone friezes carved with demons on its temple, **Pura Dalem**.

East Coast

Bali's top aristocracy, the Gegel Dynasty, ruled the island for 300 years from **Klungkung**. The highlight is **Kerta Gosa**, the Royal Hall of Justice, built at the beginning of the 18th century. Bali's supreme court, it continued to exercise its functions under the Dutch. Only very difficult cases were judged there. The walls and ceiling are painted in a style peculiar to the region with scenes designed to reassure the innocent and wring anguished confession from the guilty. They depict the dreadful punishments evildoers could expect in the Kingdom of the Dead and the blissful rewards heaped on the virtuous.

Important guests were received in **Bale Kambang**, the delightful floating pavilion alongside. Its ceiling is also richly painted in Klungkung style, a particularly finely detailed technique emphasizing primary colours and depicting personalities in profile, similar to the *wayang kulit* tradition. **Kamasan**, 2 km (1 mile) away, remains a centre for this type of painting, originally done on bark or coarse fabric. This form of art was related to the now outmoded *wayang beber* or scroll tradition of relating Hindu epics. The Klungkung ceilings were almost entirely replaced in the forties but their humour and vivacity are ageless.

Near **Kusamba** you'll notice dark lava flows, the signs of the latest eruption of Mt Agung (see p. 82). Although the people earn a living from fishing and salt production, they live a discreet distance from the sea and the menacing goddess who rules it. The thatched huts which almost merge into the black sand indicate little salt factories. The island offshore, **Nusa Penida**, supposedly home to a thoroughly unpleasant

giant, is where Klungkung used to sequester criminals in the old days. Further up the coast, **Goa Lawah** seems like the casting office for a vampire film. It's a cave which is supposed to run through the hills all the way to Besakih. You won't be tempted to explore, for the entrance is packed with thousands of bats, hanging clustered together like overripe fruit, detaching themselves to wheel over the heads of visitors. The flapping of their leathery wings and the ammoniac smell are decid-

Women bear gifts to Besakih, Bali's mother temple.

edly unsettling. The cave is holy, protected by a small shrine, and is supposed to contain a python (which feeds off the bats) and an underground river.

Many cruise ships call at **Padangbai**, a small harbour backed by hills from where the boats set out for Lombok across the strait. Scuba enthusiasts praise Balina Beach, where trips can be arranged to Nusa

Penida and Menjangan Island (north-west). These islands offer some of Bali's best diving, along with with **Tulamben** on the north-east coast.

Candi Dasa, named after its seaward temple, is fast growing into a leading beach resort but still retains its village identity with painted canoes along the shore and plenty of fishermen willing to take you out to the reef. Inland, **Tenganan**, like Trunyan (page 82), is a Bali Aga ("original Balinese") village, welcoming visitors but bound to strict *adat* practices to maintain purity. Inhabitants marry only within the settlement; they always sleep with their head towards the door; at the end of June the men do battle with pandanus leaves to draw blood as a sacrificial ritual. They weave a unique double ikat cloth called *grinsing*, where the threads for both warp and the weft are tie-dyed before weaving—wearers are protected from demonic forces. *Lontar* (palm-leaf books) of high quality are produced in the traditional manner with ink brewed from burnt nuts. In this neat little walled township the only hazards are meandering water buffalo and fighting cocks in their bamboo coops, some with feathers tinted to an unlikely shade of violent lollipop pink.

Volcanoes

On the lower slopes of Mt Batur, **Bangli** is a quiet town with a majestic temple, **Pura Kehen**. It is made up of three large sections in pink sandstone, linked by flights of steps. The first terrace is lined with statues of the *wayang kulit* type representing characters from the *Ramayana*. A splendidly hideous demon face, *kala-makara*, frightens evil spirits away from the closed gateway known as the "great exit". The inner temple shrine devoted to Brahma, Shiva and Vishnu stands crowned with an 11-tiered thatched pagoda or *meru*, while the upper

level is dedicated to the supreme god, Sanghyang Widi.

South of Bangli centre, on the Gianyar road, **Pura Dalem Penuggekan**, a temple for the dead, is covered in explicit friezes enlarging on the punishments lying in wait for sinners in the afterlife.

A small knife, well hidden, has been used for harvesting, to quieten the fears of the rice spirits.

Roads from Tampaksiring and Bangli lead directly north to **Penelokan**, "the Place for Looking" and **Kintamani**, both of which give a view of **Mt Batur**, second only to Agung as an island holy spot and still very much alive with a caldera 11 km (7 miles) in diameter, 18 m (60 ft) deep. Solidified lava has striped the mountainside down as far as **Lake Batur**, a misty stretch of changing pastel colours. Across the

lake at **Trunyan** live Bali Aga ("original Balinese") who do not cremate their dead but lay the bodies out in the open air. If you're really curious you can go there by canoe from Kedisan, but don't count on being welcomed with open arms. Bali's biggest statue, 4 m (13 ft) high, is honoured as guardian of the village; it's kept hidden away, safe from prying foreign eyes. At **Batur**, see **Pura Ulun Danu**, its towers soaring against the background of the smoking volcano. The local people have been rebuilding the temple ever since they moved out of the volcano's reach after an eruption in 1927.

Bali's holy mountain **Gunung Agung** is also its highest point, attaining 3,142 m (10,309 ft). It last erupted in 1963 after a long silence: molten lava poured down the slopes, villages blazed, crops were ruined and the entire island was smothered in volcanic ash. Almost 2,000 people were killed. For the Balinese it appeared significant that the catastrophe occurred when they were celebrating *Eka Dasa Rudra*, the greatest of their sacrificial festivals which takes place once every 100 years.

Sleepy **Amlapura** at the foot of Agung was once capital of a powerful kingdom. Badly hit by the 1963 eruption, the town changed its name from Karangasem to hide its identity from any evil spirits who might be planning a subsequent catastrophe. The volcano practically destroyed the last raja's palace and his gardens at **Ujung**, sparing only the lovely water playground he conceived in 1945 at **Tirtagangga**. Here, in perfect serenity, sweet water pours from the jaws of grotesque

---

> ### Balinese Dances
>
> *Among the most charming of Bali's 200-odd dances is the* legong, *performed by pre-adolescent girls. They wear sarongs decorated with gold and are tightly swathed from neck to waist in gold bands. On their heads are golden crowns, loaded with frangipani blossom. The girls are trained from the age of four or five to enact the story of a captured princess and her rejected suitor; they retire before puberty.*
>
> *Goodies and baddies wage battle in the* Barong *dance, where the powerfully virtuous lion-like beast Barong struggles against Rangda, the wicked witch. Rangda sometimes causes male dancers to enter a trance and stab themselves with their own krises. The Barong finally holds the day, and the kris dancers, revived by a priest, leave the performance without visible injury.*
>
> *Relatively modern, the* kecak *dance is unaccompanied by musical instruments. About 100 men perform by candlelight or oil lamp, backing the story's action with a variety of calls, croaks, chants and the rhythmic chuckling sound ("chak-a-chak") that gives the dance its name. The story is from the* Ramayana *and tells about the abduction of Sita and her rescue by two armies of monkeys.*

stone animals, lotus flowers add a blush of pink to crystal-clear pools and a banyan drops a cascade of twisting roots, providing a perfect natural altar for the modest offerings at its foot. Around, the rice glows tender green beneath the tousled heads of coconut palms.

Besakih, Bali's "mother temple" and holiest site rises high up on the south-western slopes of Agung, looking from a distance like a forest of thatched pagoda roofs rising in tiers above the quilted terraces of rice. The spot was probably sacred to the volcano god in pre-Hindu times; over more than 1,000 years it has developed into a complex of some 200 temples and shrines of which the most important is the **Pura Penataran** group in the middle. It represents one almighty God in three manifestations as symbolized by Brahma (right), Shiva (centre) and Vishnu (left).

NORTH AND WEST COASTS

This peaceful part of the island seems a far cry from the hectic hotel world of the south. In colonial days, **Singaraja** was Bali's major port; memories of this reside in the historical library and a number of impressive Dutch buildings. Several fascinating temples are to be seen in the region: Pura Beji at **Sangsit**, 6 km (4 miles) to the east is dedicated to the rice goddess and lavishly decorated with awful demons and

exceedingly lithe snakes. Near **Jagaraga**, inland, one temple has chosen a vintage boat, car and aircraft as the theme for its stone panels; another celebrates fish and fishermen. Further along the same road, up in the hills, is **Sawan**, noted for its gamelan manufacture and evening market. Back on the coast, Pura Maduwe Karang at **Kubutambahan** protects the crops grown in this un irrigated region and does so with notable gusto. The carved relief of a Balinese on a bicycle with wheels made of flowers and vegetation in a riot all around his head would be bound to please any agricultural deity with a sense of humour. **Tejakula**, 35 km (21 miles) east, has some very imposing baths, designed for horses, not people.

The north coast's attractive dark-sand **beaches** string out west from Singaraja: Happy Beach, Lovina and Kalibukbuk are the best known. En route to Menjangan Island, pause at **Pulaki** to see its temple, inhabited by a tribe of curious monkeys.

Pulau Menjangan, 5 km (3 miles) off the coast, is part of Bali Barat National Park. It's a low-lying island, with a limestone shelf on the south coast, suddenly dropping in a sheer wall to some 50 m (164 ft). The diving is fantastic; yellow, red and pink soft corals proliferate and reef fish hover in the caves.

Overleaf: Sunset turns Tanah Lot into a place for meditation.

Festivals

Two calendars coexist in Bali. According to the Hindu saka *calendar, each year is made up of 12 months of 29 or 30 solar days. The* wuku *calendar is more complex, consisting of 10 simultaneous weeks ranging from a 1-day to a 10-day week. A year is made up of 210 days, equivalent to 30 7-day weeks, also called* wuku *and beginning on a Sunday. Each day is named after a planet in the solar system. Temples and shrines celebrate their* odalan *or anniversary every 210 days, which means that there's nearly always a festival going on somewhere. Hotels and travel offices display Balinese calendars to keep you in touch with local events. Ask around, too, about local ceremonies such as tooth-filing and cremation, which is not a doleful occasion here.*

There are times when the whole island celebrates the same holiday. The main ones are as follows.

Galungan *is a 10-day festival for Sanghyang Widi Wasa, the supreme God, celebrating the victory of good over evil. The gate of each house is decorated with tall bamboo poles dangling leaves and flowers, together with bamboo altars bearing ornaments of woven palm leaves. The ancestral spirits return to earth for the length of the festival, to be honoured by a farewell feast of yellow rice on the 11th day,* **Kuningan**. *The offerings are renewed and Barongs parade with a great fanfare through all the villages.*

Nyepi *is the Balinese New Year according to the* saka *calendar, occurring on the day after the new moon of the 9th month. It's a day of silence and purification. No fires are lit and no traffic is allowed on the roads. A 24-hour curfew is maintained. At sunset the children parade banging musical instruments to frighten off evil spirits.*

Saraswati, *an annual event in the* wuku *calendar, honours the Goddess of Learning. No one is allowed to read or write and offerings are made to the* lontar, *palm-leaf books.*

The western half of Bali is clad in thick rainforest. Boats cross to Java from **Gilimanuk**, the island's westernmost town surrounded by mangrove swamps; from here you can see East Java's volcanoes on the horizon. **Negara**, on the road back to Denpasar, is a small market town which livens up in September and October for bull racing, to celebrate the end of the rice harvest.

To round off a day's travelling, arrive at **Tanah Lot** as the sun sinks. A temple dedicated to the sea spirits, built by one of the last priests to come from Java in the 16th century, it's set on an offshore islet, accessible by foot at low tide. Etched against the sky, clenched to its wind-carved rock, it symbolizes the intangible beauty and still inviolate mystery of Bali.

NUSA TENGGARA

Literally "the south-easterly islands", this mini-archipelago sometimes referred to as the Lesser Sundas stretches from Bali to Timor. Lombok and Sumbawa are major islands in the western province; Sumba, Flores and Timor are the largest to the east. Lombok draws increasing numbers of visitors, and tour operators here can arrange visits to other islands, where outsiders are relatively rare. You could also be adventurous and go it alone.

In 1869 the British naturalist Alfred Russel Wallace evolved a theory, fundamentally correct, that the archipelago was separated by a natural rift between Sulawesi and Kalimantan, continuing down between Bali and Lombok, thus forming a western group with Oriental affinities, and an eastern group linked to Australia. On each side of the "Wallace Line", the indigenous mammals were distinct. Indeed, once you cross the Lombok Strait, you'll notice a change: lush tropical landscape gradually melds into aridity, savannah and thorny scrub; rain is scantier, and prolonged droughts parch the soil. Asian animals give way to Australasian species including cockatoos, parrots and the giant monitor lizard known as the Komodo dragon.

LOMBOK

It's only four hours by boat from Padangbai in Bali to Lembar harbour, or 20 minutes by air from Denpasar to Mataram, but you'll think you're on another planet. This little island, some 80 km (50 miles) from north to south and about the same east to west, is worth discovering now, while it still retains its old-fashioned pace. The people are gentle, rather withdrawn, but they'll take time to display their masterly skills in weaving, pottery and basketry; as you approach each tiny, traditional village, children will rush to greet you with yelps of excitement. The beaches are out of this world, some well set up, others to be developed.

When the Balinese invaded Lombok, it was inhabited by the Sasak people, themselves having come from Indochina by way of Java and Bali. They withdrew into their mountains during the lengthy period of Balinese rule. Sasak culture is a curious blend of outside influences and local traditions. While the numerous Balinese who settled retained their Hindu faith, the Sasaks are

mainly Muslim, although a diminishing number clings to Wektu Telu, a more flexible form of Islamic belief found only on Lombok. A ceremonial battle, *perang ketupet,* is held every October: Wektu Telus and Hindus pray and make offerings before pelting each other with bundles of steamed rice wrapped in banana leaves. February and March witness the unique Bau Nyale festival as crowds gather to await strange "seaworms" which hatch on the reef and rise to the surface off beautiful Kuta Beach. You'll be expected to join in the traditional *gadrung* dance; nobody minds if you're less lithe and graceful than the locals, who do their best to keep straight faces while teasing participants with frangipani flowers plucked from their towering headdresses.

Mataram, the capital, has grown into neighbouring Ampenan and Cakranegara, the commercial hub, to form one town. For an overall view of the island's culture, visit Mataram's fine **museum** on Jl. Banjar Tilar Negara.

The **Mayura Water Palace** at Cakranegara, built in 1744, is the remains of a Balinese royal complex set in an idyllic park with an avenue of mangosteens. Old Dutch cannons guard the floating meeting hall which also served as a court of justice, approached over the lake by a raised

It's all go on market day.
Splash out on fruit and flowers, or
simply have your hair cut.

walkway. Nearby **Pura Meru**, the biggest temple in Lombok, was built in 1720 to unite all the island's kingdoms. It is devoted to the Hindu Trimurti, Brahma, Vishnu and Shiva. The huge wooden drums in the outer courtyard call the people to prayer.

Story has it that when the Balinese arrived in Lombok a new spring burst into life which they named *Aik Engsar* ("Appearing Water"), later modified to **Lingsar**. The temple here symbolizes Sasak–Balinese understanding and is sacred to Muslims, Hindus and Chinese alike. A special area is reserved for high-caste Hindus; in another there's a mirror, placed by the Chinese to warn off malevolent spirits. Arranged below it, stones from Mt Rinjani, the holy mountain to the north, stand swaddled in white cloth wound with a yellow sash. The adjacent Wektu Telu temple includes a pond with sacred eels which make an appearance if you throw them an offering of boiled eggs. Believers often spend several days and nights at Lingsar to pray at midnight for special blessings.

The summer palace at **Narmada**, 10 km (6 miles) east of Cakranegara, was built in 1727 by an old Balinese king. Too frail to journey to the summit of Mt Rinjani to make his offerings, he had these gardens laid out around a spring as a miniature replica of the volcano and its crater lake. The temple in the grounds, Pura Kalasa, is devoted to Shiva. Once a year ducks are ceremonially released onto the lake; amid a great deal of flapping and quacking local boys plunge in to catch them and bear them home in triumph.

Boiled eggs are on the shopping list again for a visit to the Temple of the Holy Eels at **Suranadi**, set in the hills north of Narmada among delightful gardens and spring-fed bathing places.

A trip to **Gunung Pensong**, 5 km (3 miles) south of Mataram, implies a change of menu, for on the way you'll encounter dozens of monkeys on the lookout for peanuts. A temple complex has been built here on a rocky outcrop; climb the long flight of steps for a stupendous view.

Pura Segara, a sea temple on the beach north of Ampenan, stands close to an old Chinese cemetery. The traditional Balinese boats hauled up on the sand have eyes painted on the bows to help them find their course. Lombok-style dugout canoes are made in the fishing village over the road.

A small temple sits at the top of **Batubolong**, a tall rock hollowed by the sea; visit it at evening for the rose and indigo sunset and a view over the waves to Mt Agung in Bali.

Most visitors stay in the **Senggigi** area, where there's a luxury beachside hotel establishment. The lovely sweep of sand and sea is enhanced by offshore coral gardens. Head

In Lombok the rainy west meets the drier east. Fauna and flora change but rice remains a staple.

further north for other magnificent beaches and an enticing trio of islands: **Gili Air**, **Gili Meno** and **Gili Trawangan**. A boat from Bangsal will take you out to snorkel and dive in a magical marine world of blue coral, vivid fish and delicately lovely shells. There's similar undersea life around the other islands off the south-west coast, 55 km (34 miles) from Mataram: **Gili Genting** holds top honours for anglers.

Head inland to **Sukarara**, where irresistible *songket* fabric is woven on hand looms from cotton embellished with gold and silver thread. **Penujak**, further south, is a pottery village where, among other objects, you'll discover unusual "bottomless" water pots. The water is poured into a large hole underneath then disappears when the pot is turned over. Tilt the pot normally and the water flows out through the spout—the secret is a clever inner partition. Basketry of unbelievably fine quality, renowned throughout Indonesia, is crafted in **Beleke**, west of Praya.

Dip deeper into Sasak culture at **Rambitan** and **Sade**, villages on the way to Kuta. Enthusiastic youngsters rush to welcome you and try out their English, proudly showing off their tall thatch and bamboo homes and rice barns, explaining their religion, their traditions, and introducing you to parents, *sirih*-chewing grandparents and a host of cousins. *Sirih* is a common, mildly narcotic mixture based on betel leaf and nut with the addition of other spices. The

containers for the ingredients and the stand on which they are presented are often of exquisite workmanship.

Kuta Beach, not to be confused with its better-known namesake in Bali, is an almost completely circular sweep of fine coral sand curving into a number of bays. The two main areas are **Segara** and **Tanjung Aan**. This magnificent south coast is primed for development but there is enough of it to cater to the tastes of get-away-from-it-all individualists for a long time to come.

Real outdoor enthusiasts carry exploration further by visiting traditional villages in the central north and trekking up **Mt Rinjani**. It can be dangerous in the wet season.

OTHER LESSER SUNDAS

Tourist facilities are still limited throughout the remoter Nusa Tenggara islands. The most popular are Komodo and Rinca, which attract visitors intent on dragon watching, while the Darwin to Kupang flight tempts quite a few Australians to Timor, reputed for its ikat weaving.

Sumbawa can be reached by ferry from Labuhan Lombok. A speciality of this island is *berempah*, almost bare-fisted boxing where contestants let fly at each other with their hands bound in bundles of newly harvested rice stalks. Before each match the men are rubbed with oil prepared in secret by *sanro*, or magicians, who also murmur incantations over them. There is no referee, so the happy outcome is that all participants are winners. The *sanro* also prime water buffalo for races across flooded rice fields. The finishing line is treated with magic, and it's amazing the number of beasts who baulk at the last moment, precipitating their drivers into oozing mud. It's more a test of skill for the *sanro* than the buffalo—may the best wizard win!

Flores has particularly spectacular scenery, with majestic volcanoes and mountain lakes. It is mostly Christian, though there are still several tribes practising animism. The preferred sport of Manggarai youths in the westernmost region is whip fights: protected by helmets and shields they lash out at opponents with buffalo-hide whips. A scarred back is proud proof of virility and is more likely to win maidenly approval than a smooth skin.

Along with Sumba and Timor, Flores also produces complex and highly valued **ikat** textiles. Increasing technology along with synthetic yarns and dyes have eroded the technique in some places, but Sumba, in particular, still clings to its traditional methods. Formerly only noblewomen from ruling clans were allowed to practise the craft. Nowadays the cotton is imported from Java, then sorted into bundles for the ikat ("tying") process. The yarn is bound with grass fibre, leaving some areas free to absorb dye. The first dyeing stage, using indigo, takes weeks to achieve the desired gradations of colour. In the next

stage, red *kombu* prepared from tree roots is applied; superimposition of colours results in rich purples and browns. Weaving is carried out on a back-strap loom with several women participating to produce only some 7 cm (3 in) of fabric in one day. Sometimes, on cloth of exceptional significance, yellow dye is added with a brush afterwards. The finished textile with its highly charged symbolic motifs, is imbued with spiritual power.

Stormy waters and powerful currents may make for a difficult passage to **Komodo**, between Flores and Sumbawa. Here the human population is far outnumbered by that of the local "dragons", *Varanus komodoensis,* which also roam the western coastal area of Flores and neighbouring islands Rinca and Padar, though in smaller numbers.

The Komodo dragon is the largest, most dangerous predatory lizard in existence, a scale-covered monitor with a body up to 3 m (10 ft) long, a heavy, muscular tail, snake-like head, spiked claws and fiery yellow forked tongue. These armour-clad carnivores, which have no inhibitions about eating their own eggs or each other, doubtless gave rise to Chinese myths where they are upgraded into the aerial dragon, cosmic symbol of creativity.

Ora, as they are known here, live in holes dug out of the arid land. Hatching after about 8 months' incubation, the young are agile tree climbers. They feed on a diet of other

small lizards, insects, birds' eggs, birds and rodents, working up to goats, boars and even water buffalo. Lethargic by nature, they warm to business with the sun: those slow-pacing legs can move like lightning, propelled for attack by the tail. Fearsome they may be, but superbly designed for survival in their habitat—which is less than 1,000 sq km (386 sq miles).

Seen from afar, the island appears blanketed with soft grass topped by tall *lontar* palms. From Kampung Komodo, an east-coast fishing village, you go north to Loh Liang, where accommodation is arranged. Guides (never go without one) will lead you to the dragon-spotting hideaway at **Banunggulung**, where the normal procedure is to stake out as bait a dead goat purchased on the way. Nobody really likes this method, which has killed the dragons' hunting instinct and made them increasingly fearless with humans. You're advised not to wear bright colours, especially red, which could advertise you as likely prey.

"Here there be dragons," old maps claimed. On Komodo there still are. You might feel safer sleeping on the boat.

SUMATRA

Beauty, wealth, history, everything is on a grand scale in Sumatra. Stretching 1,760 km (1,094 miles) from north to south, about the distance from Rome to Madrid, it provides more than 50 per cent of the national income from its natural riches: tin, coal, oil, bauxite, gold, rubber and palm oil. Huge saline swamps occupy much of the east coast; a mighty volcanic range, Bukit Barisan ("Marching Mountains") strides down the island near the western coastline. Of about 100 volcanoes, 15 are still active. The population of 30 million seems sparse against the vast background of marshland, jungle, high country and lakes, and a transmigration policy has been implemented to move people here from Java. They are offered land, adequate housing, one year's supply of basic foodstuffs and help from experts in setting up their farms.

Many Sumatrans are Christians, including the Batak people around Lake Toba, the principal area of interest for tourists. International airlines fly in to Medan, North Sumatra, while cruise ships anchor in the city's port of Belawan.

ACEH

The province of Aceh occupies the northern tip of the island. The area was part of the Buddhist Srivijaya empire in the 7th century, then was included in the Hindu Majapahit empire of eastern Java until the early 16th century. With the arrival of Islam, the sultanate of Aceh was established, the first Muslim stronghold in the archipelago. When Marco Polo visited the region in 1291, he reported that the inhabitants had all been converted to the law of Muhammad "owing to contact with the Saracen merchants who constantly frequent them". It was the first part of Indonesia to be in touch with the outside world, a centre for Arabic and Asian trade which reached its zenith in the early 17th century.

Dutch occupation was fiercely resisted but in 1873 Banda Aceh was taken; 25 years of open warfare ensued, followed by frequent rebellions until Aceh was granted the status of a special district in 1956. Still staunchly Muslim, the province welcomes visitors respectful of a near fundamentalist code of behaviour. Local languages are based on Arabic, which most Achinese used to be able to read and write.

The capital, **Banda Aceh**, contains a fine colonial building in the old **Governor's residence** (1880); it managed to survive the long, bitter years of the Aceh War, which lasted intermittently from 1873 to 1942, re-igniting in 1948 during the Indonesian War of Independence. Dutch visitors find memories of times past in the **Kerkhof**, or churchyard, resting place for some 2,000 soldiers.

Imposing **Baiturrahman Mosque**, near the river, was built by the Dutch as a peace offering to replace a structure burnt down at the start of hostilities. Take a rest in the gardens and contemplate the multiple styles of the façade.

Little remains of **Taman Sari**, the royal pleasure gardens, apart from a 17th-century structure erected for the sultan's Malay wife. Known as Gunongan ("Imitation Mountain"), it is set against artificial hillocks created to console the princess with memories of her native land.

The excellent **Aceh State Museum** displays regional costumes, jewellery and weapons. Aceh has a long tradition for the manufacture of fine jewellery in precious metals, daggers, swords, and exquisite embroidery.

This uncrowded province also offers a number of **beaches** close to the capital, including Lhoknga, Ujung Bate and Lampu'uk, reputed for its shining white sand. Take a wrap to cover up after your swim, since scanty clothing gives offence.

NORTH SUMATRA

It was tobacco that first brought riches to this province when, back in the middle of last century, a Dutch planter called Nienhuys set up an estate near the Deli River, producing smooth, sought-after "Deli leaf".

The provincial capital, **Medan**, is the country's fourth international gateway after Jakarta, Denpasar and Batam. The gracious old town is astonishingly cosmopolitan, with a large Chinese community. It positively throbs with commerce—the harbour of Belawan handles 65 per cent of Indonesian trade. The Medan industrial and cultural fair is held annually from the end of March to early May.

There's a group of old **colonial buildings** near Jl. Jen. A. Yani, including the town hall, the Bank of Indonesia and the city post office, all late 19th- and early 20th-century. The best souvenir shopping is along the same street. Pasar Ikan, the fish market, has become a batik centre.

Istana Sultan Deli, also known as the Maimoon Palace, was built in 1888; the old sultan, though pensioned off, still lives there. You can go in as long as there's no ceremony in progress. The throne is a dazzling sun-burst of yellow silk. A mixture of Arab, Indian and European influences, nearby **Mesjid Raya**, the grand mosque, has a beautifully painted dome and doors. **Gang Bankok Mosque**, dating from the 17th century, is the oldest in Medan.

Visitors are sometimes admitted to the richly decorated **Chinese mansion** on Jl. Achmad Yani.

Towards Belawan, off the main road, **Kota Cina** village offers an excavated site where 9th-century Buddhist statues as well as Tang, Sung and Ming coins and pottery were uncovered in the 1970s. The **Crocodile Farm** displays some of the most dangerous species in the world, from tiny ones paddling around in plastic basins to giants drowsing half-submerged in a pool. Don't lean over the fence to make their acquaintance, they can move like lightning.

Lake Toba

The faster and less scenic route to Lake Toba passes through tobacco fields and extensive oil and rubber plantations to **Pematang Siantar**, North Sumatra's second largest city. Pause along the way to see latex being bled into tin cups tied to the trees. Alternatively, take the 6-hour drive via **Brastagi** on the Karo highlands, a mountain road past sweet-scented cottage gardens full of roses and dahlias. The climate produces delicious fruit including the *marquisa,* a mammoth passionfruit, and superb vegetables exported in bulk to Singapore. The town is overlooked by two volcanoes, Mt

Arab, Indian and European cultures have all influenced Medan. Following pages: Lake Toba, home to the Batak people.

Sibayak, 2,094 m (6,870 ft) and Mt Sinabung, 2,451 m (8,042 ft). It used to be a retreat for Dutch planters and still has some attractive colonial houses.

Lingga, 16 km (10 miles) on, is a traditional Karonese Batak village with stilt houses, some over 200 years old. Go accompanied by an Indonesian—the villagers don't always welcome outsiders. The **Raya Museum** on the Brastagi–Kabanjahe road displays Batak objects. **Sipisopiso waterfall**, plunging 110 m (360 ft), is an hour's walk off the main road at Tongging, between Kabanjahe and Pematung Purba. There's a 200-year-old teak **Batak tribal house** at Pematang Purba before the road joins the main highway at Pematang Siantar for the direct trip through to Prapat, on the very edge of **Lake Toba**.

Glittering aquamarine when the sun shines, green and menacing under a stormy sky, the lake is North Sumatra's jewel-like centrepiece. It's hauntingly lovely by moonlight, especially if one of the local Batak choirs is practising. Their beautifully blended voices ringing out across the water seem to bring old magic to life.

One of the highest lakes in the world, 853 m (2,800 ft) above sea level, Toba was created by volcanic explosion. It covers 1,300 sq km (500 sq miles) and is approximately 426 m (1,400 ft) deep. In it lies **Samosir Island**, 635 sq km (245 sq miles) in area, 30 minutes' boat trip from Prapat.

Samosir is the cradle of Batak culture. Their legends relate that the various Batak tribes all descended from a god hero born on a holy mountain near Toba, though it would seem they really originated in Thailand and Burma. Living only in the highlands, they developed a warrior culture involving frequent inter-village warfare and were the "head-hunters" of Sumatra, practising ritual cannibalism. They attach mystic significance to the number three. Magic books, *pustaha laklak* (literally "bark books") written in their dialect with many Sanskrit words, deal with three subjects: preserving life, destroying life, and divination. Like the Hindus, they believe in three aspects of God, represented by three colours, white, red and black, symbolizing the high, middle and lower worlds. These are the colours painted on their houses and woven into their clothing. Nowadays the majority are outwardly Protestant Christian, first converted in the late 19th century. They have a natural gift for music and are extraordinary chess players.

Most visitors to Samosir Island stop first at **Tomok** to visit the royal cemetery with stone tombs about 400 years old. Huge banyan trees shelter the ancient graves.

Ambarita is a picturesque little spot with old Batak houses set high on poles pre-soaked in mud to strengthen them. Dwellings and rice storehouses follow the same design, with front and back walls slanting outwards, ornamented with carvings. The sway-backed roofs are made of sugar-palm fibre or—nowadays—corrugated iron, and a carved buffalo head is set at each end of the gable. Only the three Batak colours are used, and the whole construction is built without nails. There are no interior walls: mats are hung to give privacy. About eight related families occupy each house. Once a boy reaches puberty he leaves to live in a special "bachelors' house" with others of his age.

Ambarita also has an old judgement place with a stone table and seats where chiefs used to meet. If things went badly, it was off with the criminal's head on the spot.

Simanindo presents an outstanding Batak house and puts on dance performances which usually include a demonstration of *si gale gale* puppets. These almost life-sized marionettes are made to "dance" in jerky, uncannily human movements. Originally they were used in death rituals and destroyed afterwards.

Lake Toba offers a big, week-long festival in June with canoe racing, dancing, processions and music.

Nias

It's a long, pleasant drive through ricefields, plantations and hilly country covered with secondary jungle to the little port town of **Sibolga**. From there you can charter a boat to Nias island, but it's a tough trip. The direct flight from Medan is easier.

The usual greeting on Nias is *Johol*, "Strength". The island is populated by former warriors and head-hunters who still preserve traces of their megalithic culture. An Islamic traveller first described them in AD 851. Since then they have been Christianized, but their lush, hilly little island, set like an elongated shield in the Indian Ocean, is so isolated that old ways of life still flourish.

Bawamataluo, Orahili and Hilisi-maetano are a trio of fascinating villages accessible from the port of

Traditional storehouse in Lingga village, a Batak stronghold still true to its old ways.

Telukdalam. Of them **Bawamataluo** ("Sun Hill") is the best, perched above Orahili at the top of 480 (they'll be graven into your memory!) stone steps. Stilt-built houses surround a main square with stone chairs linked by bamboo chains to wooden carvings inside the houses. The chairs are for the ancestral spirits, attached to their living families

whom they survey and protect. Sometimes skulls are placed under the seats. On paving stones around the square are old carvings, which used to "advertise" the trade of the householder living there.

The **chief's house** is suitably grand and spacious, decorated inside with rows of pigs' jaws. The pig holds a predominant position in Niah culture, facilitating the introduction of Christianity rather than Islam, which outlaws the pig. Society was divided into three classes, the nobles, free commoners, and priests; a non-class of slaves built the houses fronting the square like galleons riding a sea of stone. They were placed close together so that their occupants could run from one to the other without descending to the ground in case of attack.

In Bawamataluo and Hilisimaetano traditional war dances are performed in the square. The Tulo Tulo warrior dance is a Hollywood spectacular of yelling, stamping, charging men, some of them dressed in leather armour adorned with spikes imitating crocodile teeth. Their big black necklaces used to be the sign of a successful headhunter—and not so long ago on Nias a man had to produce a head to merit a bride! Two heads gave the right to two wives, and so on. The women in yellow and scarlet, richly bedecked with gold jewellery, dance demurely in lines.

Another tradition of Nias is stone-jumping, which used to be ritual training for manhood and battle. In the old days the pile of stones was spiked with bamboo and the men hurled themselves into space with a weapon in one hand and a flaming torch in the other to clear it. They're more cautious these days.

Lagundi, on the coast between the port and the hill towns, is a quiet Islamic settlement with a good surf beach.

WEST SUMATRA

Volcanoes, gorges, luxuriant forest and blue-green lakes make this province of almost 50,000 sq km (19,300 sq miles) seem like a vast natural park. It's inhabited by the Minangkabau people whose matrilineal system means that all wealth and family names pass through the female line. The most important male in domestic affairs is the mother's eldest brother, who is responsible for the well-being of his brothers, sisters, nephews and nieces. Since women own the land and property, the men travel a great deal to set up businesses in other parts of the archipelago.

The Minangkabau are strongly Muslim, and life centres around innumerable mosques fronted by big open fish and bathing pools, and huge houses (*rumah gadang*) with horn-shaped roofs resembling the

She dances quietly in gold and scarlet. Her ancestors were the headhunters of Nias.

horn-shaped headdresses of the women. They say their name means "victorious buffalo". Verbal and poetic, they have a strong literary tradition. The economy relies largely on coal, cement, rubber, cinnamon and tea.

The coast is hot, the highlands cool and airy. Accommodation is generally adequate, and there's a good hotel at Bukittinggi, the touring centre of the region.

Padang, the clean, prosperous provincial capital, a two-hour drive from Bukittinggi, is famous for its super-spicy cuisine. Well-groomed horses pull open cabs with a coquettish air, red pompoms nodding on their heads as they step it out. Government departments are housed in a modern example of a *rumah gadang,* as is **Adityawarman Museum**, which displays traditional costumes, old tools and weapons and Chinese ceramics (closed Mondays). **Taman Budaya**, the arts centre opposite, usually has Saturday afternoon cultural performances.

An old quarter with rundown Dutch buildings is now mostly occupied by the Chinese population. The port of **Muara** is crammed with smallish craft and from here you can go to the **Mentawai Islands** where the patrilineal society is dominated by extraordinarily strict and complicated taboos. The beach at **Bungus**, about 20 km (12 miles) south of Padang, offers good sand, swimming and windsurfing. Boatmen will take

you out to picnic on the little atoll that sits so invitingly in the bay.

South of Padang lies the enormous **Kerinci-Seblat reserve**. Weird but unconfirmed reports have come in about an *orang pendek* (a mysterious hairy hominid), the *cigau* (half lion, half tiger) and the *kuda liar,* a wild horse which appears to terrify villagers. What certainly exist are rhinos, tigers, tapirs, elephants, clouded leopards, sun bears and cobras, and the great hornbill, found only in Sumatra. Travel is most difficult in the wet season: October to December, and April. There's accommodation at Sungaipenuh. Allow 10–12 hours to drive from Padang.

Bukittinggi and Vicinity

From Padang, pass by **Lake Singkarak** or cross the magnificent **Anai valley**, the river running swift and clear below. You might be lucky enough to experience a tropical electrical storm, with cobalt flashes of lightning making the traditional Minangkabau houses seem even more theatrical, floating like Noah's ark in a watery world of paddies.

Daily downpours are so heavy in **Padangpanjang** that West Sumatrans call it "rainy town". **ASKI**, the Conservatory of Minangkabau theatre and music, puts on regular performances. Along the

Women control the wealth in West Sumatra. Their headgear is shaped like the house roofs.

road you'll see working monkeys, specially trained to pluck coconuts from the palms. Stop a while in **Pandaisikat**, a hand-weaving centre and the place to find excellent wood-carvings in scarlet and gold.

Bukittinggi itself, at an altitude of 930 m (3,050 ft) is encircled by three volcanoes, Sago, Singgalang and Merapi. Indonesians call it *Kota Jam Gadang*, roughly translated as "Big Ben town", because of the old clock in the market place. The Dutch built **Fort de Kock** in 1825; it's now a park where people go to watch the sunset.

The **museum** is housed in a Minangkabau house near the **zoo**, which is not especially appealing but does have some rare Sumatran animals. Many visitors choose to walk through **Ngarai Sianok**, a canyon just out of town. **Kota Gadang** village, on the other side of the canyon, has a reputation for fine silver filigree jewellery.

Beyond Kota Gadang at **Lawang Peak**, you have a superb view over rice fields all shades of green, the flooded areas shining like mirrors in the sun, and over **Maninjau**, a large crater lake. The road to Maninjau winds round 44 hairpin bends—it might be a good idea to have your vehicle blessed by one of the local magicians who'll give a thorough treatment to wheels, motor, dashboard and all. Once there, you'll find swimming, fishing and boating.

Nglau Kamang, 8 km (5 miles) to the north-east of Bukittinggi, is a big cave splodged in pop art patterns by green and pink mosses and haunted by squeaking bats. It's easy going but you'll need a torch.

Batusangkar, south-east, seat of a 14th-century Minangkabau kingdom and real cultural heart of the area, is a quiet country town. Head east to **Pagaruyung** for archaeological remains including the royal graveyard and, further along the same road, a grand new *adat* palace built according to age-old instructions and used as a museum.

Pariangan, on the slope of Mt Merapi, is supposed to have been founded after the great flood. The village revolves around an *adat* house and mosque, in the time-honoured Minangkabau way.

In July and August you may see rafflesia blooming at **Batang-palapuh**, north of Bukittinggi. The huge red and white flower has a repellent smell, akin to rotting meat.

The road to Medan runs through 3,000-ha (7,415-acre) **Rimba Panti reserve**. The office there will provide a guide to take you into the forest and point out many kinds of monkeys, honey bears, flying squirrels, a whole carnival of butterflies and birds—and maybe traces of a tiger.

RIAU

This wealthy province on the east coast extends into a confetti of off-shore islands; it's located on one of the world's oldest sea routes. Many of the islands are tiny: out of an estimated 3,000, only 743 are named.

Bahasa Indonesia, the country's Malay-based language, was born here. As Buddhist power eroded in the 13th century, Malay realms grew in strength on both sides of the Malacca Straits, leading to the foundation of the Malacca Kingdom in 1402. Portuguese takeover in 1511 was followed by jostling for power between the Dutch and British with the Dutch eventually gaining the islands. Today most of the people are Islamic Malay.

The island of **Batam**, only 20 minutes by boat from Singapore, has soared in importance as an arrival point for Bintan, the largest island in the group. Oil, gas and related industries were the basis of Batam's riches, and it is now a duty-free zone. Overseas investors have been encouraged, resulting in the implantation of residential, sports and hotel districts.

Holidaymakers usually continue to Bintan where **Tanjungpinang**, the main town, is a traditional stilt city built over water. From here there's motor boat and ferry transport to many of the other islands for great beaches, surfing and snorkelling. Sunken wrecks dating from World War II, particularly at **Mantang Island**, add spice to the diving scene.

On the Sumatran mainland, **Pekanbaru**, capital of the Riau province, lives from oil and has a large foreign population. The surrounding area remains adventure territory where it's easy to come across elephants, tigers, rhinoceros and wild boar.

SOUTHERN PROVINCES

Capital of the province of the same name, **Jambi** exports timber and rubber. From there you can journey up the Batanghari, the longest river in Sumatra.

In the South Sumatra province, **Palembang** is the island's main oil export centre; many of its buildings rest on piles sunk into the Musi River. This has always been one of the trading hubs of the eastern world, reaching its historic peak in the 11th century. Four hundred years before that, a Chinese Buddhist visited and noted its intellectual and commercial vitality, the multitude of languages spoken and a harbour crammed with ships. Some glimpse of the Chinese heritage remains in **Klenteng Kwa Sam Yo**, a temple ornamented by a series of narrative wall paintings. Islamic importance is commemorated in **Ki Gede Ing Suro**, a complex of eight 16th-century Muslim tombs.

The river rules this city's life, raising and lowering the raft houses with its ebb, swelling broadly in the rainy season. *Perahu ketek,* flat bamboo boats, ferry you between Seberang Ulu and Seberang Ilir, the upper and lower parts of town. You might prefer to cross by the landmark **Ampera Bridge**, starting-point for viewing the hectic river life, a noisy jumble of boats, waterside houses and floating markets.

Two museums, **Rumah Bari** and **Rumah Adat Bayumi**, display traditional objects as well as samples of *songket*, glorious silk fabric overwoven with gold and silver thread. Wedding ceremonies are gorgeous affairs, harking back to Palembang's Hindu heritage, as do the Srivijaya dances—the girls wear glittering golden headdresses and elongate their fingers with golden nail-covers.

Don't miss a long **river trip** to be drawn into a life-style which has remained unchanged for centuries. North-west of Palembang, hidden away in swamps and jungles, the nomadic pygmy Kubu people occasionally venture from their forest hideaways to trade in the villages.

The province of **Bengkulu** on the south-west coast is a quiet little territory rarely visited by the outside world. Sir Stamford Raffles based himself in Bengkulu City from 1818, keeping the Dutch at bay and boosting the pepper trade. **Fort Marlborough** contains a number of old British graves. Very forlorn the names seem, read on crumbling tombstones under a tropical sun. **Sukarno's house** here dates from the nine years he spent under Dutch arrest from 1933 on.

In this area you may sight *Rafflesia arnoldy*, named for Raffles who, apart from being lieutenant-governor, was a dedicated botanist. The world's biggest flower feeds on insects, is a mammoth spread of orange-red spongy bloom noted for its repulsive odour and can be tracked down if you're in the region at monsoon time. It seldom grows in the same spot twice, so ask around.

Lampung, Sumatra's most southerly province, easily accessible from Java, is geared for an increasing number of visitors with international-standard hotel accommodation in the capital city, Tanjungkarang. A beautiful forested landscape, great beaches, inviting islands and Krakatau visible just off shore are some of the draws—not to mention elephant football matches!

Way Kambas Reserve on the east coast contains a unique elephant training centre funded in part by WWF. Close to 300 wild Sumatran elephants plod along happily in an expanse of waving giant grasses, co-habiting with tigers, tapirs, monkeys, and birds in tremendous variety. Ride an elephant to explore their natural habitat and, from observation towers, witness the moving spectacle of their mating. December and January are the months for this extraordinary experience.

Marvellous textiles, particularly yellow, gold-embellished *tapi*, come from here, further enhanced, for ceremonial occasions, with a decoration of coins, symbolic of prosperity. Study it more closely at the **Lampung Museum** in Tanjungkarang and pay a visit to the memorial erected to the Krakatau eruption. The volcano is easily reached by boat from here.

KALIMANTAN

Fewer than 10 million people inhabit the vast spread of tidal swamps, mighty rivers and jungle-clad peaks that form Kalimantan, occupying roughly three-quarters of the huge island of Borneo. The Malaysian states Sarawak and Sabah, together with the Sultanate of Brunei, make up the north-western part of the island.

Rich in petroleum, natural gas and coal, gold, diamonds and other precious stones, Borneo is geologically ancient. The volcanoes died out thousands of years ago. Here are some of the world's last great rainforests; protection of the wildlife heritage is now of international concern after logging, clearance for crops, and fire probably destroyed several rare species. There's a wide variety of fauna and flora, although most of the big predatory mammals never roamed here. Instead there are rarities like the rhinoceros hornbill, a sacred bird to some Dayak tribes; royal pythons; the beguiling flying frog that spreads its fingers to help it float; clouded leopards; the small nocturnal lori with dark rings around its eyes like a short-sighted old gentleman in a woolly overcoat. *Kalang,* a species of buffalo originating in China, has adapted to the swampy environment to swim from one grazing ground to another.

The most ancient monuments yet found in Indonesia, dating from the 4th–5th centuries, have been uncovered in the Mahakam River area of East Kalimantan. Remote though it was from the Greco-Roman world, Ptolemy recorded a description of Borneo in his 2nd-century atlas; Roman beads have been found which must have arrived with one of the drifts of eastern traders who came seeking precious metals, sandalwood, camphor and other exotic treasures along the coasts and up the arterial waterways. These same accessible areas were Islamized from the 15th century on, while the interior remained untouched.

In the days of headhunters, Borneo's history was interrupted by an adventurous Englishman, James Brooke, who invested his legacy in a yacht, sailed from India to Brunei and, after using his army background to help master an uprising was, in the 1840s, made first governor, then raja of Sarawak—himself and his heirs in perpetuity. Brooke died in England in 1868 but the "white raja" dynasty continued to 1946 when Sarawak and Sabah became British Crown Colonies before being incorporated into Malaysia in 1963.

Indonesia's part of the island is divided into four provinces: West, South, Central and East Kalimantan. Tourism centres around Banjarmasin, capital of South Kalimantan, and Balikpapan in the east, but excursions can be arranged into the central area. Local tour agencies are particularly helpful, and adventure's there to be had in jungle trekking and white-water rafting. The easier travel experiences include trips down the Barito River and the superb voyage up the Mahakam River to meet the Dayak people, the original inhabitants of Borneo, erstwhile headhunters, today friendly and fascinating hosts. Arrange to fly and boat out of Benjarmasin to Tanjung Puting National Park to sight the orang-utan in their tropical habitat.

BANJARMASIN

Lying below sea level on a network of marshland and connecting waterways that rise and fall with the tides, the town is located where the Martapura River merges into the Barito. In the dry season the Barito is saline from the sea to the "floating city"; when the rains come it laps against the raft verandahs of the stilt dwellings which line its banks. The river *is* Banjarmasin. The river people hold up their children to see you—you'll have a sore arm from waving and a sore throat from shouting "Hullo".

The only land monument to visit here is the modern, much-revered **Mesjid Raya Sabilal Muhtadin**, a mosque named after a major Islamic work by Al Banjary, born at nearby Martapura in the early 18th century. His fame is such that Muslim pilgrims travel long distances to visit. During Ramadan there's a fantastic cake fair near the mosque—religion is strict but not restrictive.

You'll need at least two river trips to appreciate Banjarmasin. In the late afternoon, putter seaward some 12 km (7 miles) in a motorboat, pausing while the propellor is cleared of trailing water hyacinth, to **Kaget Island**. This is a haunt of the proboscis monkey, *Nasalis larvatus,* known locally as *bekanten.* These alluringly droll creatures with their long, pendulous red noses swing from the trees like roisterers on the way home from a particularly wild party. You'll probably see them returning from a day's foraging for their favourite food, the fruit and young leaves of *pidada,* found in mangrove swamps. Membranes between their toes help them paddle from one food supply to the next. This is an endangered species, protected since 1972 and scheduled to become South Kalimantan's official mascot—they are threatened by poachers who sell them off for huge sums to pet-hunters. Deprived of their familiar diet, the monkeys usually die.

South Kalimantan has diamonds, sifted out of yellow mud, offering a glimmer of hope.

BANJARMASIN

As you glide from their hideaway the setting sun patterns the quiet river with golden scrolls. Another island, **Kembang**, is the home of the long-tailed macaque monkeys who put on a great turn for visitors courteous enough to arrive with peanuts and tropical fruits.

Get up early for Banjarmasin's **floating market**—it starts at 5 a.m. All the merchandise is sold from boats, and there are even "floating cafés" where you choose your breakfast pastry with a boat-hook.

On the way to the diamond mines at Martapura, pause at Banjarbaru to visit **Lambung Mangkurat Museum**, built in sweeping traditional style with a statue of a hornbill under the roof. Malay people inter-

Life in Kalimantan depends on the waterways, the link between all villages and markets.

marrying with indigenous Dayak in about the 6th century formed the basis of the Banjar whose weaving, pottery and household objects are well displayed.

In this part of the world *galuh* means a beautiful and virtuous girl; the word is also used for the diamonds found at **Martapura** mine pits, for to call a diamond by its real name would be to frighten the precious, timorous stone away. You're not supposed to sneeze at the mines, nor eat sour or fermented food, nor stand with your hands on your hips, a stance considered uncouth throughout Indonesia. Coarseness of any kind would send *galuh* into hiding. In spite of precautions she remains a distant dream for many of the workers who stand hip-deep in yellow sludge, scooping up mud and water in bamboo baskets for women to carry away

on their heads for washing and sorting. Months may pass before a stone is found. No one knows how potentially rich the mine is. In local workshops, craftsmen apply inherited skills to polish the gems. You can buy the results nearby, together with Kalimantan's *sasirangan* cloth, originally made by holy men and accorded the power of being able to cure diseases. Created by a tie-and-dye technique, the dominant colours are yellow, green, red and purple.

As well as the possibility of visiting Central Kalimantan from here, you can also travel by air-conditioned bus from Banjarmasin to Balikpapan, passing through palm-oil, rubber and cacao plantations and long stretches of rainforest. The easy option is to fly.

BALIKPAPAN

The capital of East Kalimantan is Samarinda, 60 km (37 miles) up the Mahakam River, but Balikpapan is the major centre, a clean, wealthy city just 3 km (2 miles) from the busy airport. The first thing that strikes you is that the traffic is sparse, calm and disciplined. Some hundreds of expatriates, including a number of French, work for the big petroleum companies sited inland and offshore—if you fly over the area at night you'll be able to locate Balikpapan by its candelabra of oil flares. "Kaltim", short for the province's Indonesian name *Kalimantan Timur*, is one of the

country's richest regions. A mere 1½ million people live in an area the size of England and Wales combined.

Call at the **Altea Benakutai Hotel** even if you're not staying there; not only is it a landmark with a well-earned reputation for excellence, it also contains a very good display of Dayak objects and provides information about river tours on the Mahakam as well as land trips to sight Kaltim's rare black orchid. The travel agency within the hotel

complex can arrange packages which include accommodation here, transport to areas of interest and Dayak cultural performances, even overnight stays in a Dayak "long house".

"Dayak" covers over 200 tribes which moved further and further inland as Malays settled the coast: Islamization would have deprived them of pork, their favourite food. A handsome, pale-skinned people reputed for their "magicians", they used to practise headhunting to bring

Water for drinking and ablutions is drawn from the Mahakam, the artery of East Kalimantan.

strength and security to their villages. Great concern was lavished on the heads which were smoked before being placed in a carefully decorated setting, then honoured and pacified with offerings of food and tobacco so that the vital energy contained would harbour no ill will but feel happy in its new environment. Unfortunately, the spiritual energy in a head became exhausted after a certain time, so the supply had to be renewed. Nowadays, in ritual, a coconut often stands in for a head. There are pockets of primitive tribes deep in the interior, skilled in bushcraft, living from jungle fruits and hunting with darts and blowpipes. Perhaps, very rarely, headhunting rituals still occur, but certainly not among the Dayak you'll meet. The older people still have elongated earlobes, tugged to shoulder-length by the weight of metal earrings. Many tribes pay special reverence to the hornbill which plays a part in their myth of creation; the male and female of the species gave life to rivers, sea and human beings in their struggle for the holy, waxy buds of the Tree of Life (the rice plant).

The **Mahakam expedition** begins at Loa Janan, just upstream from the timber town of Samarinda. You'll find a comfortable houseboat with a minimum crew of three; two to take turns steering plus a cook already planning amazing feats in the galley—from a classic *gado-gado* all the way to madeira cake. The occasional relative, friend or villager in need of transport will also hop on from time to time. At every stop people flock to see you, waving and calling out, holding up their babies, trying out their knowledge of your language, enthusiastic about your attempts to speak theirs. The grand old river tubs have a simple shower and toilet; you sleep on deck on perfectly comfortable mattresses with mosquito nets. During the day they're spirited away to make a lounging and dining area.

There's nothing to do. Gliding upriver, you'll gradually lock in to the life of the jungle, floating past villages where everything depends on this mighty waterway. Morning mists maturing into sleepy high noon, the washed blue, red and weathered timber of stilt houses, a glint from the minarets of tiny mosques, evening prayer calls competing with the dart of kingfishers: this is the highway of East Kalimantan. The boat will pull in at **Tenggarong**, once seat of the Kutai sultanate. An Art Deco palace, built for the sultan in 1939 by the Dutch, displays old royal paraphernalia as well as Dayak arrows, beads and carvings and Chinese porcelain.

A tiny crowd awaits at **Muara Muntai**, a neat little town with wooden boardwalks for streets. Buy suitable gifts at local shops (your guide will advise) to present at the Dayak welcome ceremony later. Then you're making your way between shoulder-high swamp grasses, home and hunting ground for thousands of marsh birds. If the water level is sufficient, the boat continues across Lake Jempang; if not, you'll transfer to a motorized canoe, occasionally stopping to disentangle roots of water hyacinth from the propeller.

Tanjungisui is one of the homes of the Banuaq Dayaks. News of your arrival has travelled ahead, and you'll be formally challenged at the entrance to the village. Your guide will have taught you the appropriate reply, a promise of peace, and, at the call to enter, he'll slash the twine decorated with leaves which guards the entrance. You'll be guest of honour for refreshments, Dayak-style, and the traditional dancing which follows.

Many variations are available to the basic trip. You could visit **Lake Semayang** to sport with its freshwater dolphins. Or take a motorized canoe up narrow riverways, through thickly crowding jungle, perfectly reflected in the still water, silver ripples spreading behind. You can also go ashore for a jungle trek. There'll be sumptuous meals including freshwater shrimp, fish caught in heart-shaped traps staked to the river bed, tiny "finger" bananas, rosy sugar bananas and delicious pineapple. By the end of the trip you'll feel that you, too, are part of the generous life of the majestic Mahakam.

Monkey Business

Sometimes there are very special travellers aboard flights to Indonesia. This pampered élite flies first class, well supplied with bottled spring water, yoghurt, and lush tropical fruit. Apart from solicitous "aides de camp", several members of the cabin crew are delegated to respond to their every whim, taking it in their stride when the VIPs decide to career on all fours down the aisle. Following the international flight, the passengers are discreetly transferred to airforce flights before boarding speedboats for the final leg of their journey. The welcome is in keeping with their status as privileged Indonesians, although totally out of proportion to their size. Baby orang-utan are returning home.

They were kidnapped from their mothers before they were able to fend for themselves and smuggled from their leafy environment to Asian ports, to await transport to Europe and the United States where they fetch thousands of dollars. Now these diapered infants are as traumatized as human children.

The "forest people", which is what their name means in Malay, are found only in North Sumatra and Borneo. Only 10 to 20 thousand survive, and the species is in danger of dying out. Orang-utan are protected by international agreement, but for some people they remain prestige pets. When they're confiscated or owners decide voluntarily to part with them, they're sent to Indonesian rehabilitation centres to get back into the swing of being a full-time ape.

Visits can be arranged to both centres: Bukit Lawang, 80 km (50 miles) west of Medan in North Sumatra; and Camp Tanjung Harapan, Central Kalimantan—as well as forest walks, there are old Dayak tombs in the area.

SULAWESI

Sulawesi stretches out four peninsulas like the crumpled petals of a giant orchid; Portuguese navigators mistook these trailing wings for separate islands. The name *Ponto dos Celebres* ("Cape Infamous"), which they gave to a particularly dangerous stretch of coastline, became attached to the whole island and for centuries it was spoken of in the plural as "the Celebes".

Each peninsula is administered as a separate province. Four ethnic groups live in Sulawesi Selatan (South Sulawesi): the Minahasa in the north; the Toraja people in the central region; and in the south-west the Makassanese and Buginese, the "sea gypsies" of old mariners' tales. They are among the most fearless sailors in the world, and from their number came some of the dreaded pirates of the Java Sea—daring, swarthy-skinned men whose tall-masted schooners, known as *pinisi,* chilled with fear the foreign spice merchants.

Arabs, Spaniards, Portuguese, British and Dutch all sailed this way. A proud monarchy, the Sultans of Gowa, struggled for generations against foreign powers intent on forcing their way through to the limitless riches of the Moluccas, famous throughout the world as the "Spice Islands".

The capital is Ujung Pandang, a lively trade port which used to be known as Makassar. One of its exports was macassar oil, essential hair-grooming aid for many a Victorian gentleman, whose liberal usage resulted in that much-derided drawing-room accessory, the antimacassar.

High in the mountains to the north lies Tana Toraja, where villages of enormous, boat-like houses are scattered over the countryside. According to local mythology, Torajanese ancestors descended to earth from heaven on two mountain peaks. In fact, they probably came by sea from South-East Asia; the strange, saddle-roofed houses commemorate the boats which brought them. Unlike their Muslim neighbours to the south, many are outwardly Christian, but the ancestors' teaching, *aluk todolo,* is nonetheless reverently followed and amounts to a death cult. In some months (August to October) there are several funerals a week. They are occasions for mingled mourning and rejoicing.

Parts of this large island are practically inaccessible, jungle-covered mountains, fascinating for their flora and fauna and for the remote tribes which inhabit them, but seldom visited by outsiders. Most visitors spend a short time in Ujung Pandang where there's a busy airport with flights to many other destinations; from there, usually by road, they head up to Tana Toraja.

UJUNG PANDANG

Long known as Makassar, today's Ujung Pandang has been a communications and commercial centre for nearly 500 years. The fortress, **Benteng Ujung Pandang**, was first raised in 1545 by one of the kings of Gowa. The earthen walls were replaced by brick some 80 years ago. In 1667 it was taken over by a Dutch admiral, Cornelis Speelman, who changed the name to Fort Rotterdam in honour of his own birthplace. Complete reconstruction ended in its becoming the seat of civil government for the Netherlands. The storehouses, with elegant colonial verandas, housed cargo prior to shipment to Batavia and on to Europe; nowadays, transformed into **La Galigo Museum**, they contain excellent displays of ethnological and historical objects. **Taman Budaya**, the Conservatory of Dance and Music within the compound, welcomes spectators during rehearsals.

The fortress dungeon was, for 26 years, the prison for one of Indonesia's earliest freedom fighters, Prince Diponegoro, exiled here until his death after leading the Java War from 1825 to 1830. His grave and monument lie in a small cemetery on Jl. Diponegoro.

Three **temples** along Jl. Sulawesi are reminders of the city's large Chinese population. Tuan Hou Gong, "Temple of the Heavenly Queen", contains a statue to this patroness of sailors. Long Xian Gong,

This little piggy went to market...all trussed up on its owner's back.

"Temple of the Apparition of the Dragon", a late 19th-century structure, honours Ian Mu, Mother of the Immortals and the patron gods of jewellery and of prosperity. The Chinese used to visit the nearby restored Temple of the Association of Guang Dong if they had to appear for court hearings.

South of the fort, at Jl. Mochtar Lufti 15, a Dutch enthusiast has assembled a celebrated collection of rare **shells and corals**; he also maintains a long-established nursery of rare Indonesian orchids. Further south, visit **Tenunan Sutera Alam**, the silk factory on Jl. Onta Baru; glorious fabrics are dyed and woven on the premises.

Evening is the best time to visit **Paotere harbour**, when the superb *pinisi* schooners at their most romantic, tinted by the sun sinking into the Makassar Strait. Real addicts sometimes take the 153-km (95-mile) trip to Bulukumba to see the boats being built at Biri Cape. Near Paotere old graves and a few other remains recall the Tallo kings who co-ruled with Gowa monarchs and were influential in the spread of Islam.

The former seat of the Gowa monarchy is at **Sungguminasa**, 11 km (7 miles) from the city. A dignified wooden palace, now the **Ballompoa Museum**, has some pleasant exhibits, but the real marvels, priceless royal regalia including a gold crown and sacred, gold-handled kris, are not on public display. Not far from Sungguminasa lie several royal tombs, including that of Sultan Hasanuddin (died 1679) who fought with exceptional bravery against the Dutch. **Katangka Mosque**, built during the first years of the 17th century, rebuilt and restored in modern times, is surrounded by royal graves.

Effigies of ancestors crowd the balconies of Toraja's cliffs.

NORTH TO TANA TORAJA

From Maros take the turn-off to **Bantimurung**, where colourful butterflies dance over the waterfall. The less fortunate of their number are displayed in a small museum. The limestone mountains in this region are threaded with caves, some containing prehistoric rock carvings. At **Leang-Leang** the cave wall is marked with blood-red handprints believed to date back some 5,000 years.

Along the road north you'll notice picturesque Bugis houses set on stilts, with thatched roofs of palm fibre. The verandas are edged with carved wood, the paint faded to harmonies of blue and green dappled by the light filtering through crowding banana plants. The tall foundations used to be a protection against wild

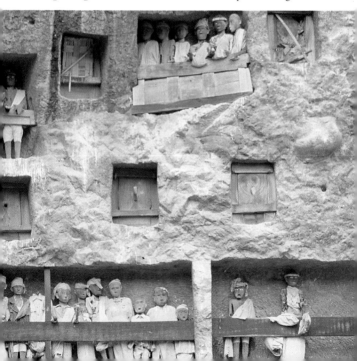

animals and still serve to cool the interior. You may glimpse women working small looms in this basement area, especially in the afternoon. Stop if you can, to watch them weaving fine silk cloth. Widths are narrow because of the size of the looms but the colours are rainbow-vivid and hard to resist. This area is also known for its dry rice, grown without irrigation and considered so outstanding that it's exported all over Indonesia. See the harvesters tying the stalks into bundles for transport, and threshing it in the fields in three-sided shelters. Rice fields alternate with fish pools, both harvested twice a year.

Pare Pare, 55 km (34 miles) north of Ujung Pandang, has a natural harbour where cruise liners often put in. From here the road climbs into the hills. There's a view of Kandora and Gandang peaks where the celestial ancestors are supposed to have set foot, and the Erotic Mountain, so-called because of the sensual moulding of its valleys and slopes resembling a supine female form. A gateway in traditional boat shape marks the entry to the Torajan lands.

A cool, green and pleasant land set about 700 m (2,297 ft) above sea level, **Tana Toraja** is rather cut off from its neighbours by mountain ranges and has maintained its cultural identity to the present day. Roads are still fairly poor (and sometimes downright awful) and much of your enjoyment will come from exploring on foot. The majority of people have assumed Christianity and there are some Muslims, but many find no conflict in continuing to practise their old religion, *Aluk Todolo*, the worship of their ancestors' spirits.

Torajans traditionally spend their lives amassing wealth with the sole objective of providing for the finest funeral possible. High on their list of assets is the "coloured" buffalo marbled in shades of pink and black which can fetch up to a million rupiah. The buffalo are slaughtered at the funeral service, along with pigs and chickens. Tall monoliths in stone are traditional hitching-posts for buffalo sacrifice.

Because of the cost of a funeral, the deceased are often kept for years, carefully watched over night and day by a member of the family. Until buried, the person is referred to as "ill" and the spirit is considered potentially malicious. Human sacrifice was once part of the ritual, which can last for up to ten days. The Torajans recognize many gods but only one supreme being, *Pong Matua*, creator of all things. Everything owned on earth is thought transported to the afterlife or *puya*, situated "somewhere to the south".

Two basic religious ceremonies are practised, both involving animal sacrifice. *Rambu solo* (soul ceremony) includes burial and grave cleansing. *Rambu tuka* (god ceremony) brings good fortune to a new house or expresses gratitude for an abundant harvest.

Society is made up of three classes: nobles, a predominant middle class, and commoners. Thousands of people may attend the funeral of a noble, and up to 200 buffalo are killed. Foreign guests are quite welcome to witness the feasting, music, singing and dancing, as long as they observe the proprieties and offer a small gift. In the old days, complete villages were built for the occasion and burnt afterwards.

At the end of the ceremonies, the body is hoisted up a tall bamboo scaffold to its resting-place in a niche dug out of the mountainside. These graves are sometimes called "houses without kitchens". Even more bizarre are the balconies tacked on to the front of the burial cliffs, where jack-wood effigies of the dead, dressed in clothing they might have worn in life, stand stiffly in rows, staring with wistful, painted eyes over the rice fields. Their garments can be renewed, provided a buffalo is slaughtered.

The 400,000 Torajans make their living from the cultivation of rice, vegetables, cloves and coffee. Some still live in the traditional boat-shaped houses decorated with buffalo horns from past sacrifices. According to ancestral law, the houses must face north, towards the race's place of origin; they can easily be moved from one place to another. Only local building materials are allowed: wood, rattan and bamboo; nails are forbidden. Marvellously symmetrical designs adorn walls and beams: white for the human skeleton, red for blood, black for death and yellow for the radiance and benevolence of God.

Unlike the *tonkonan* (house), the *alang* or rice barn faces south, representing the underworld ruled by Pong Tulakpadang, who supports the earth. It is set on round, not square pillars, to keep rodents at bay. The first floor is used as a meeting place, the second for grain storage. Decoration is less stylized, depicting ordinary household and agricultural tasks.

Makale is the district capital but **Rantepao** the main centre for tourism. **Kete Kesu**, 4 km (2¹/2 miles) south-east of Rantepao, is a traditional village incorporating a craft centre. Behind lies the cemetery with coffins shaped like boats, pigs and buffalo, and effigies surveying you from a vantage point. At **Londa**, directly south of Rantepao, village children will lead you into the catacombs—a macabre experience—to glimpse skeletons by flashlight. Take binoculars and a telephoto lens for photography when you visit **Lemo** where funeral effigies (*tau tau*) stand on a balcony, immobile guardians of tradition. At **Bori**, 8 km (5 miles) north of Rantepao, see the *rante,* stone buffalo sacrifice megaliths placed in a circle. **Palawa**, to the north-east, is an old settlement with excellent traditional houses, while **Sadan** is known for its weaving. Several villages such as **Karassi**, complete with megaliths, were constructed in recent years specially for the burial of nobles; once they would have been destroyed after the ceremony but nowadays they are left standing, and members of the family occupy some of the houses. There are many similar points of interest which can be reached only on foot—ask at your hotel if there are any ceremonies in the offing. You'll see shy children dutifully caring for great, doe-eyed buffalo and riding on their backs through the watery acres of the rice fields.

Don't miss **market** days, involving dozens of buffalo, hundreds of pigs, the big ones carried squealing on litters, small ones joggling along in slings on their owners' backs. In Rantepao the animal market is a short distance from the general market where you'll find palm wine sellers toting their wares in hollow bamboo, sizzling heaps of chilis, aromatic tobacco stacked in piles and supremely good basketry.

NORTH SULAWESI

The long, north-eastern peninsula ends in a series of small islands reaching towards the Philippines. It's mountainous and volcanic, with great, inviting sweeps of white beach. Flying to Manado, the capital, you see the tossing heads of innumerable coconut palms—this is the main copra-producing area of Indonesia. The people are basically Minahasan, westernized (traditionally pro-Dutch), Christian, and very

outgoing towards foreigners. In outlying areas, though, you'll be a real curiosity. The biggest draw is exceptionally good diving at Manado and around the nearby islands of Manado Tua, Siladen and Bunaken.

Manado feels, looks and is a rich little town. The boutiques sell fashionable Japanese-made clothes, goldsmiths proliferate, and there's a large Chinese population. Cheap minibuses with winsome names

("Super Love", "Good Father") follow set routes to service the city; you might prefer a more leisurely promenade in a *bendi*, a two-wheeled horse-cart. A big event in mid-February is the Toa Peh Kong Chinese festival held near Manado's

Regional markets offer their own specialities, along with a bewildering profusion of produce.

Buddhist temples, where entranced men pierce their tongues with needles in a ceremony dating back to the 14th century.

Diving is centred just out of town at the Nusantara Diving Club, **Malayang**, where attractive beach cottage accommodation is available. Divers are advised to bring personal items such as depth gauges and divers' watches. Reef life and structure is particularly rich, and there's

30-metre visibility. You'll see pyramid butterfly fish, scorpion and shrimp fish, visit submerged caves, meet baby whales and hitch rides on amiable turtles. You can arrange here a visit to the sea gardens off **Bunaken Island**, now internationally acclaimed as among the best in the world, with a huge drop-off, ocean caves and deep gullies, rare and brilliantly coloured marine life and unpolluted seas. Deep waters bring you within sight of manta rays, sharks, and old wrecks from World War II. For a break from diving, there's mangrove swamp exploration near Bunaken Bay and native-style tuna fishing from outrigger canoes. No rods are used, just line and a hook baited with chicken feathers.

Drive through giant coconut and nutmeg groves to **Bitung**, the seaport at the foot of bush-covered Dua Saudara mountain on the east coast. There's a fishing fleet and fish market near the main harbour where the copra boats put in.

Permission is needed from the P.P.A. (Nature Conservation) office, Jl. 20 Mei, Manado, to visit **Dua Saudara nature reserve**. Carry your own water and buy insect repellent at local chemists for protection against vicious red mites. You can expect to see black macaque monkeys, dwarf buffalo, pygmy squirrels, maleo birds nesting in areas of volcanically heated sand, tailor ants which glue leaves together to make their nests, and the strange archer fish which shoots insects down with jets of water. Whales often play offshore. Jeep access is possible in the dry season (December to February inclusive); you can take a boat from Bitung to Batuputih village on the reserve's northern tip.

Kema Beach makes a fairly pleasant outing. Drive on through the nutmeg town of **Karegesan**, stopping maybe to buy *palat manis*, a local sweet made of nutmeg flesh. **Airmadidi** has the best collection of *warugas* (pre-Christian tombs) in the area. Bodies were placed inside in sitting positions, together with their belongings. Offerings are still made to important tombs. Even older *warugas* are found on the way to Sewangan, where the Japanese Army built tunnels during World War II.

Weathered, unpainted wooden houses on stilt foundations with rows of pot plants in glassed verandas give an oddly suburban look to villages on the road to **Remboken** and **Tondano Lake**. Further inland, **Tomohon** is a mountain settlement where you'll see cloves drying in the sun.

Tara Tara, a Minahasan art centre, is the place to see local dancing and hear a bamboo band. Enquire in advance at the tourist office about performances which are not regular but can be arranged. At **Tinoor**, stop for the view and, if you dare, for the local culinary specialities—bush-rat and dog-meat. **Tasik Ria**, about 20 km (12 miles) from Manado on the west coast is a beautiful undeveloped beach.

MALUKU

Formerly known as the Moluccas, the original "Spice Islands" of romantic history, these minor land masses directed the course of world history. Cloves, cinnamon and nutmeg were the lure which sent European explorers steering into the unknown. For centuries the prized commodities found their way to the West via Indian and Middle Eastern trade routes; the desire of European monarchs to possess the source of such boundless wealth was the first step towards discovering the Indies. Many of Maluku's estimated 999 islands are still littered with reminders of a power struggle which began more than 1,000 years before the Portuguese invaded the islands in 1512. The Spaniards wanted control of the clove trade, too, as did the Dutch, who took over in the 17th century. The Dutch East India Company was originally built on trade in spices, paving the way to Netherlands domination of Indonesia. Forced cultivation was

abolished only in 1863. Nutmeg is still one of the prime exports.

Ironically, Maluku today sees few outsiders. Located on a line of volcanoes in a transition zone between Asia and Australia, culturally part Malay, part Melanesian, these islands lie well off the main tourist routes. Only 1.7 million people live in the entire area, many of them converted to Christianity under Portuguese and, later, Dutch influence. Wild life is rich and varied, including rare butterflies and many kinds of parakeet; entrancing coral gardens fringe the islands. You'll meet with an enthusiastic welcome, but don't expect to see many other visitors, except on Ambon, Ternate, and the Banda group.

AMBON ISLAND

Most of the 200,000 people live in coastal villages, headed by a raja. Hilly **Ambon**, the provincial capital, overlooks a bay. To learn about local history, visit **Siwa Lima Museum** in the southern outskirts of town. On Karang Panjang hill, a statue commemorates the heroism of Martha Christina Tiahahu, who fought valiantly against the Dutch and is honoured with a special ceremony on July 2. The Dolan memorial was named for an Australian soldier who died covering the retreat of his compatriots during World War II. More than 2,000 Allied servicemen lie in the **ANZAC War Cemetery**, some 5 km (3 miles) from the city centre.

Waai, a village 31 km (19 miles) to the north, boasts a pool swarming with eels, said to have been created by a raja who threw his spear to find a suitable spot for settlement. The eels, considered sacred, are supposed to leave when any disaster is heralded for the island. They are tempted from their underwater cavern by gestures from the keeper and a sprinkling of boiled egg. The biggest one, with a handsome red stripe is, of course, top eel.

The Darwin to Ambon international yacht race, a 600-nautical-mile test of courage pioneered in 1973, has become an annual event, giving rise to endless welcome ceremonies including traditional dances, hard-fought village rowing contests and, wildest of all, *becak* races. Ambonese cheer on the pedalling competitors and their passenger as Australian yachties risk their necks in a mad pedi-cab sprint to the finishing line. Increasing overseas participation in the yacht race is likely to make the fun even more fast and furious.

Little **Saparua Island**, 2 hours away by ferry (50 minutes by speed boat), produced a great hero, whose statue also stands on Ambon. Thomas Matulessy was given the name *Pattimura*, "Gentle Heart", when he spared the son of a Dutch commander. Later betrayed and

Fragrant spices: nutmeg, cinnamon and cloves, offered wealth to European adventurers.

executed, his last words to his captors were: "Have a pleasant stay, gentlemen." **Duurstede** fort on Saparua, restored and housing a museum, is a reminder of past misunderstandings.

TERNATE

Cloves drew the Portuguese and Dutch to Ternate, the capital of the North Maluku group. And the heady scent of cloves and nutmeg still fills the air. All over the island, remains of old forts lie hidden beneath encroaching vegetation. **Ternate town**, on the slopes of a smoking, rumbling volcano, is an important shipping centre, quieter than Ambon. At Afo, just out of town, see the world's most ancient clove tree, 400 years old.

BANDA ISLANDS

One of Indonesia's deepest oceans, the Banda Sea, washes this group, 160 km (99 miles) south-east of Ambon. Here are the famous Maluku **sea gardens**, crystal waters bright with coral and tropical fish. In 1619 almost the entire population was killed by Dutch attempts to control the spice market. The land was put in charge of VOC employees known as *perkiniers*, delegated to supply nutmeg at Company prices. Remains of their dwellings and churches exist, and nutmeg still grows on two of the largest islands—Banda, and Banda Neira.

IRIAN JAYA

Last, loneliest and largest of Indonesia's provinces, Irian Jaya occupies the western half of New Guinea as well as a number of off-shore islands. It represents 21 per cent of the country's area. This is the land of superlatives: grandiose swamplands, towering mountains, slow-moving rivers looping to the sea. Snow glitters year-round on several of the highest peaks, with Puncak Jaya at 5,030 m (15,503 ft) soaring into a world of alpine meadows, montane forests and icy crags.

The region lies east of the Wallace Line, in the area of Australasian flora and fauna, and the variety of wildlife is infinite. Huge salt-water crocodiles raise their snouts in the sluggish rivers. Tree-kangaroos with cleverly designed "rain-capes" like an old-time French *gendarme* grow their fur downwards from the shoulders to help the water run off. Cuscus, resembling possums, swing in the trees; spiny anteaters forage for insects. Death adders top an impressive list of poisonous land and sea snakes; spiders include a fearsome whopper which can kill and eat a bird; some 75,000 varieties of moths and butterflies add sparkle to the air. The cassowary bird, a handsome giant with indigo plumage, can disembowel even a human enemy with its claws but has the disarming trait of relying on the male to incubate the eggs. Best known of all is the bird of paradise. Many old-time Europeans believed that they had neither feet nor wings because specimens were shipped out with these removed. The females are clad in discreet and tasteful brown; it's the males which develop glorious trailing plumage to strut before the little women in the mating season.

BIAK

Some flights pause briefly on this island, a vital link during the Pacific War. At **Goa Binsari**, there's an infamous cave complex where 6,000 Japanese were trapped and burnt alive by American forces. The monument to their memory is a place of annual pilgrimage for Japanese compatriots.

Fire-walking, once forbidden by the Dutch, is now recurring, especially in **Adoki**, a village 11 km (7 miles) from Biak town. Men prove their marital fidelity by walking

Pigs and stone axes are still currency among the Dani people in the isolated Baliem Valley.

across red-hot coral rocks—but scorched soles, indicating deviation from strict virtue, are not altogether uncommon!

There are beautiful beaches on the island and although few visitors linger, those who do can make for the tiny **Padaido Islands**.

JAYAPURA

The provincial capital is a pleasant, orderly town, 40 km (25 miles) from its airport. Between the two is a **memorial** on a hill, with a simple plaque stating: "Here stood the headquarters of General Douglas MacArthur and Task Force Reckless during the Pacific War, 1941–1945." After the National Heroes' Cemetery, you'll pass alongside **Lake Sentani** where fishermen and potters dwell in stilt houses. The lake is inhabited by strange saw-fish, which smash at their prey with long bills. Both the **State Museum** and **Cendrawasih University Museum** display Irian artefacts; they were endowed with important exhibits by John D. Rockefeller.

Turn left at the foot of the hills in Entrop for the **crocodile farm**, one of many in Irian Jaya. A road on the right runs to Hamadi Beach, site of the first Allied landings.

An American, Richard Archbold, was the first outsider to glimpse the "hidden valley", in 1938.

BALIEM VALLEY

There's no real reason for prolonging a stay in Jayapura; most visitors are intent on proceeding to **Wamena**, entry point for the Baliem Valley. You'll fly over coiling rivers, steaming, knotted jungle and remote missionary airstrips to this little town set at 1,600 m (5,250 ft). As your plane lands they'll be sounding a siren to warn locals off the runway. Many of the businesses here are run by South Sulawesi people. Don't miss a visit to the **market** for an introduction to regional foodstuffs and customs and your first real glimpse of the Dani.

There are at least 225 distinct tribes in Irian Jaya. New ones surface from time to time, and linguists have struggled to classify the enormous number of languages into five related families. Ample opportunity for exploration and research exists in this tropical fastness. The highland Dani, a Stone Age people dwelling in an idyllic valley near Wamena, were undiscovered until the 20th century. They still live in thatched huts, cultivating *ipere* (sweet potato) and rearing pigs. In the past they indulged in flamboyant and short-lived warfare, more out of boredom than anything else. Dani conflicts were mostly ritualistic, rarely lengthy or bloody, and were usually postponed when it rained—as they were an opportunity to show off it was vastly preferable that one's feather and fur regalia remained unspoilt by bad

weather. Their presence was revealed to the outside world only in 1961 when they became the subject of a superb film, *Dead Birds*. Often called "the gentle warriors", the men spend part of their time protecting the women planting in the fields, and the rest tending the long gourds which they train into *holim* (penis sheaths). Nowadays the sheaths are held in place with rubber bands; this meagre wardrobe is sometimes supplemented by a shell breastplate, a selection of feathers and cuscus hair

for decoration. These same courteous warriors weave armbands and skirts for their wives. Both girls and matrons fabricate a special net bag, *noken*, worn by a band across the forehead and falling down the back. It's knit from bark fibres rolled on the thigh, coloured with clay and vegetable dyes, and serves as a carrying bag as well as a kind of shawl. Unmarried girls are clad in a low-slung pandanus grass skirt; married women wear a darker fibre skirt.

All is not untroubled paradise.

Schools, hospitals and the introduction of new crops are slowly changing the way of life.

Despite the efforts of government and missionaries, more medical care and schooling is needed; dietary habits have resulted in poor nutrition and a number of preventable diseases. The "gentle warriors" of Irian's Shangri-La valley have a short life span.

Out of Wamena by road, visit **Akima** village to see the mummy.

Pigs are cherished pets, slaughtered by bow and arrow for marriages and funerals.

Something like 250 years old, locked into a squatting position and smoked to skin and bone fragility, it is the human remains of Werapak Elosarek, an erstwhile mighty warrior. It's kept in the chief's hut to be lovingly but casually displayed. Some 5 or 6 such mummies exist in the valley.

Jiwika, an administrative centre, has a small market on Fridays and Sundays, set up on trestles inside two long sheds. Stay at La'uk Inn, to be in the centre of things. There's a brine pool nearby up a steep hill, where crushed banana trunks are soaked then dried and burnt to extract salt. But it's a tough climb, and a desperately slippery descent after rain. At **Waga-Waga**, north, there's a limestone cave inhabited by bats—take a flashlight, follow the guide's instructions and watch your footing when the bats fly out. You

can trek through this peaceful "lost" land, crossing woven swing suspension bridges, maybe heading for magnificent Baliem Gorge.

Should you have occasion to be present at a Dani funeral, you'll see numerous pigs slaughtered close-up with bows and arrows, then cut into pieces with bamboo knives to be steamed in earth ovens. The mourning women cake their faces with yellow clay; the men are magnificent in pig grease and soot. The livestock is paid for in stone axes and net bags—money means very little here; most Dani recognize nothing larger than a 100-rupiah note. When you finally tear yourself away, express your gratitude for an unforgettable experience with school exercise books and pens for the children.

ASMAT COUNTRY

Michael C. Rockefeller, son of New York governor Nelson Rockefeller, worked on the film *Dead Birds*, shot in the Baliem Valley in 1961. He died on the Casuarina Coast of southern Irian Jaya later that year under circumstances which have never been clarified. He and a companion were stranded in a capsized boat at the mouth of the Siretsj River while two others went for help. Tired of waiting, Rockefeller set out to swim ashore. Sharks, crocodiles or drowning could have caused his death, but cannibalism couldn't be ruled out. After the incident the Asmat region was closed to visitors, but now it's gradually opening up again. Check with your hotel, travel agent or the police in Jayapura to see if you need a special travel pass for Asmat. It should be a simple matter.

This world of alluvial swamp is reputed for its extraordinary carving. An Asmat myth recounts how the Creator grew lonely so carved figures out of wood. Then he made a mighty drum. As he beat the first strokes on the drum, the figures came to life and peopled the world. The Asmats still believe that carving connects this world to the next; artists and their families are supplied with food delicacies, especially sago worms, which are particularly relished. Sago is the staple, and the fronds are employed to make wigs and woven waistbands and to embellish masks used to frighten the spirits of departed ancestors to Safan, the land of the dead.

Missionary influence, destructive in some parts of the Pacific, has been sensitive and beneficial here. In 1963 the Indonesian government, in an attempt to eradicate headhunting, cannibalism and inter-tribal warfare, forbade traditional feasts and the carving of associated objects. Catholic intervention, specifically from the Crozier Fathers of Minneapolis, helped save existing craft objects and protect the identity of the people, resulting in the opening of the important Asmat Museum of Culture and Progress at **Agats** in 1973. Located on the Aswetsj River, this mission centre was founded only in 1950 and serves as a base for visitors.

Magnificent carvings in the **museum** include canoe prows, shields, spears, paddles, symbolic canoes or "soul ships", bowls, masks, and utensils for the preparation of sago, mainly carrying stylized designs of water, snake tracks, flying foxes and cuscus tails, and painted white, yellow, red and black. The Asmat themselves often paint around their eyes with ochre to look more fearsome, like the black king cockatoo. Although stone was rare and precious in these tidal mudflats, some carvers had access to metal pieces washed ashore from shipwrecks, converting them to use as tools.

Also in Agats, visit **Pusat Asmat** to observe artists at work and see tribal performances. Small motorboats can take you further up-river, depending on the tides. **Syuru** is a fascinating village with traditional dwellings; maybe dare it across the mudflat to appreciate the *jew*, a communal long house.

WHAT TO DO

SPORTS

Swimming. There are dozens of beaches, white sand, black sand and somewhere in between. Major hotels have pools which non-residents can use for a fee, and towns of any size offer a public pool. Inland, there are plenty of opportunities for a cold plunge in rivers and lakes.

Surfing. Several of the best surf beaches are accessible only by boat. Batu Keras (near Pangandaran, West Java) is recommended; the bay has strong parallel currents. Pelabuhanratu, south of Bogor (Java) has great waves—go beyond the Samudera Beach Hotel. From Bali, surfers sometimes take a boat to Blambangan peninsula (East Java), reputedly rewarding. On Bali itself surfing is good at Nusa Dua and Sanur (October–March) then at Kuta Beach and Ulu Watu (April–September), the latter only for the experienced.

Diving. Scuba gear can be rented at Pulau Seribu (Thousand Islands), Jakarta's main seaward resort, which has a whole island for divers. Pulau Pencang and Pulau Panaitan (Ujung Kulon, West Java) are reportedly good. Off Bali, dive near Padangbai and at Nusa Lembongan on Nusa

You don't have to be grown up to toss a line into the well-stocked fish ponds.

Penida island. At Tulamben near Kubu, there's a wreck where the fish swim about goggling at *you*. The Riau Archipelago is excellent: beaches, coral, wrecks from World War II. Near Manado (North Sulawesi) you'll find glorious diving, also speedboats and sailboats for hire. Adress enquiries to the Nusantara Diving Club, Malalayang 1, P.O. Box 15, Manado. Ambon has two marine reserves, Pulau Pembo (less good because of the local habit of dynamiting for fish) and Pulau Kasa (best September–March). There are hundreds of islands in the vicinity accessible by hired boat. Watch out in this area for stinging coral, sea urchins, poisonous stone and cone fish and "butterfly" fish.

Boating: Local boats are always available for hire, and there's organized rental at developed beaches. For "social" boating, contact the Jakarta Offshore Sailing Club, Kotak Pos 230/KBY, Jakarta, or the Yacht Club (P.O.R.A.).

Mountaineering, trekking, riding. Much of Indonesia is in the "ring of fire", and the Indonesian Vulcanological Service keeps a weather eye on the most active volcanoes. Best for climbing are Gede and Pangrango (West Java), Semeru and Kelud (East Java) and Rinjani (Lombok). There's also horse-riding and hiking or walking in most high country resort areas. Jakarta has an International Saddle Club at Mampang (Jl. Warung Buncit Raya). For most nature reserves you need permission from the Directorate of Nature Conservation and Wildlife Management head office, Jl. Juana 9, Bogor, West Java. Check with your travel agent whether you'll need a Travel Letter *(Surat Jalan)* to enter Kalimantan and Irian Jaya. You should always call on the village headman *(kepala kampong)* in outlying areas to make your presence known. He will help with accommodation and guides.

General sports with great appeal for Indonesians are table tennis, badminton, bowling, football, basketball, baseball and jai alai. Jakarta has horse and greyhound racing. There are several golf courses such as Ancol, Jakarta, and the Bogor links (West Java). Sports Clubs all offer swimming facilities and can give information about tennis, bridge, squash and other activities; most have restricted membership. Ask at the Executive Club, Hilton Hotel, Jakarta for advice. Chess is a mania around Lake Toba, North Sumatra.

Among **spectator sports** are the bull races on Madura; bull fighting in East Java and at Koto Tinggi, Koto Baru and Kota Laweh villages near Bukittinggi, West Sumatra; ram fighting near Bandung. Kite-flying is a favourite pastime—express your enthusiasm and you'll have friends in no time, all helping build you a custom-made model. In and around Yogya (Central Java) you can bet on scorpion fights—prospective winners are on sale in the main street. Don't try to pat the favourite.

ENTERTAINMENT

Hotel reception desks, tourist offices and their publications are the best source of information about *wayang*, dance and festivals. Be sure to ask for the Directorate of Tourism's *Calendar of Events*, giving the exact dates of main attractions in all areas.

In **Jakarta**, traditional dances are performed nightly except Monday at the Jakarta Hilton's Balinese Theatre, from 7–8 p.m. Hotel Borobudur Inter-Continental offers Friday evening performances. There's always something going on at Taman Mini; you can be sure of dance Sundays from 9 a.m. to 2 p.m. Ancol Art Market has performances every evening and Sunday morning.

Dayak village, Kalimantan. Even in remote places, performances can be arranged for visitors.

This is the land of dance, courtly and gentle.

Wayang kulit (leather puppets) can be seen in action the second and last Saturday of the month at the Central Museum and may be presented Sunday mornings (check first) at the Wayang Museum in Batavia. The Central Museum is the place, too, to hear Sundanese (West Java) gamelan music, weekly on Sunday mornings.

Wayang orang or *wayang wong* (dance drama with or without masks) is performed Tuesday, Wednesday, Friday and Sunday at the Bharata Theatre, Jakarta, beginning at 8.15 p.m. and finishing about midnight.

In **Yogyakarta** you can enjoy gamelan rehearsals at the kraton Monday and Wednesday mornings, and court dancing Sundays at 10 a.m. For *wayang kulit* go across the street from the Ambarrukmo Hotel to Yayasan Ambar Budaya, Monday, Wednesday and Saturday 9.30–10.30 p.m. The Ambarrukmo Hotel itself has a nightly cultural programme in its 7th-floor Borobudur Restaurant. The Ayastya Art Institute, Gedong Kiwa III, has *wayang kulit* Sundays through Fridays at 3 p.m. and *wayang golek* on Saturdays, same time. The latter is also played at the Nitour Office (Jl. K.H.A. Dahlan 71) daily at 10 a.m. for two hours.

In Yogya, too, the Ramayana Ballet performs at Dalem Pujokusuman every Wednesday and Friday at 8 p.m. and at THR (Public Amusement Park) daily at 8 p.m. Among "set" festivals, don't miss the Ramayana Ballet at Prambanan (near Yogya) monthly, May to October at full moon, or extracts from the Ramayana epic at the Cendra Wilwatikta open-air theatre (near Surabaya, East Java) at Pandaan, twice monthly from June to November.

In other large or middle-sized towns, refer to readily available regional brochures; in villages just follow the music and the voices. Local audiences are irrepressible. They don't need theories about participation, they *live* the whole thing. In all areas where there are no planned performances you can arrange one for yourself, preferably as part of a group to cut down expense, through the local tourist office, hotel or, if you're really away from it all, village headman.

Western-style **nightlife** exists in the cities and at resorts on Bali. Hotels have cabarets with live bands and there are discos, mainly in Jakarta and Surabaya.

There are plenty of **movies**, censored for sex and violence if they come from overseas. Local fare is enlightening about day-to-day life and magical beliefs. Only large cinemas are air-conditioned. Hotels play video films with Anglo-American sound tracks and offer television which is often an excellent introduction to sightseeing or local culture. **Massage parlours** exist, along with associated participatory sports.

SHOPPING

The country produces a bewildering choice of goods, varying from one region to another.

Jakarta. In Sarinah Department Store, Jl. M.H. Thamrin, you can choose from batik, puppets, masks, basketry, snakeskin shoes, bags and jackets, paintings, carvings and jewellery. Alternative wide-range shopping spots are the Ancol Market (you'll have to bargain) and the Indonesian Village at the Hilton Hotel. Naturally, many objects are more expensive in the capital than they are in their place of origin.

GKBI, Jl. Jenderal Sidirman 28 is another good address for hand-drawn, stamped and printed batik. Many shops in the Blok M area on Jl. Melawai IV, V and VI at Kebayoran Baru carry batik fabric, garments and gifts (toys, purses, table sets). Some *kain ikat* fabric finds its way to Jakarta.

Best spots for antiques are Jl. Surabaya, Jl. Agus Salim and Jl. Kebon Sirih Timur Dalam. Good Dutch and Chinese objects are less common than they used to be but oil lamps often turn up along with coins, masks and spears, old kris handles, antique sarongs, hand-embroidered *kebayas* (blouses), jewellery, musical instruments, wooden and parchment puppets, flat, increasingly rare *klitik* wood and leather puppets and *sirih* (betel) sets with pots and betelnut cutters.

Kalimantan diamond jewellery is on sale in quality boutiques. Indonesian opals are gaining celebrity, especially the "Java black". Don't despise useful and decorative objects in tin, with a lovely soft sheen.

West Java. Handcarved *wayang golek* puppets come in various sizes; souvenir models are frailer than those used in performances but nonetheless beautifully finished.

Cirebon and Tasikmalaya have distinctive batiks, and palm-leaf weaving reaches a high standard. There are also *angklung* musical instruments in bamboo.

Central Java. Yogya's batik is strictly brown and white; Solo's uses brown, cream and indigo. Pasar Klewer (Solo) is Java's best-known fabric market. Painted *wayang beber* scrolls are on sale at the Solo kraton. Embossed leather goods start off beige and ripen to darker brown; check the stitching when you buy. Kasongan village specializes in pottery—flap-eared elephant money-boxes for the big savers and friendly chickens for small-timers. Kota Gede village produces filigree silver inspired by batik motifs. Curio hunters will have fun in the Pasar Trewindu (antiques market), Solo, and the Malang market (out of Yogya).

Paintings can be seen and bought in galleries near the Fine Arts Academy in the western part of Yogya. Seni Soto Art Gallery is the biggest in the city. Reputed artist Sapto Hudoyo has a studio in his residence on Jl. Solo.

East Java. Madurese batik is prized. There's a lot of faked brassware on sale in Surabaya, and the main street is a source of cheaply priced consumer and electronic goods.

The choice of souvenirs is mind-boggling, and different for every region.

Bali. Woodcarving, from the superlative to the trite, especially at Mas, and examples of bone, shell and horn carving. Study Balinese painting at the museum in Ubud in order to understand its development before buying. Balinese silver is airy and appealing, as are colourful masks in light wood. A *barong* on the wall might keep away the evil spirits and bring you back one day to Bali! Sandalwood fans are cheap and useful. You'll also see bright umbrellas and banners, fun for patio use, baskets and, for the really committed, stone carving. "Antiques" tend to be suspect—the word doesn't make much sense to the Balinese who produce objects today much as they did 400 years ago.

South Sulawesi. Glorious hand-loomed silks are made north of Ujung Pandang and sold there or in the city. Filigree silver is often in the shape of *pinisi* schooners. Jl. Sompaopu has plenty of shops selling gold and other metal jewellery as worn by Buginese and Makassanese women. Toraja produces hand-loomed cotton with patterns of buffalo. You'll also see lots of bamboo work, including manuscript holders, lampshades, flutes and reproductions of traditional houses. Kete village has several antique shops with old carvings, incense pots, betel-nut paraphernalia and so on. Superlative hats and baskets as well as big knives and choppers in Rantepao market—don't grasp the sheath when you draw these for a look.

North Sulawesi. Carved wood including some ebony. Clove, nutmeg and mace are aromatic souvenirs.

West Sumatra. Silver and needlework at Kota Gede and lovely handwoven cloth embroidered with gold and silver from the villages of Pandai Sikat and Silungkang. You'll also see superb embroidered marriage canopies and wall hangings. Cane fish-traps are intriguing and cost only a few pence.

North Sumatra. Wood carvings including the *tunggal-palaluaan* wand used by magicians and objects shaped like powder-horns for carrying magical substances are found on Samosir. There are also old carved elements from Batak houses or models of the houses themselves. Almanacs, bark and bamboo books are produced as souvenirs. Cotton fabric in scarf-like lengths is a speciality.

Nias islanders carve small wooden figures for ceremonial use. Or maybe you'd like to invest in a bib-shaped "head-hunter's necklet"—just the answer for those exasperating occasions when you haven't a thing to wear!

Superlative fabrics are made throughout **Nusa Tenggara**; the basketry on Lombok, in particular, reaches an exceptional standard, tightly and finely woven into traditionally shaped objects which would enhance any decor. Lombok also produces pottery—heavy, but you can arrange to have it shipped.

Excellent furniture is manufactured throughout Indonesia but in **Kalimantan** you have the opportunity to select from precious tropical timbers indigenous to the island. The diamond mines have shops nearby offering a selection of jewellery. Dramatic fabrics on sale have an uninhibited "contemporary" look and could be used for curtains and cushions. The bright bead necklaces, so becoming with resort clothes, are unfortunately strung on fragile thread.

Net bags, woven from fibre by the women of **Irian Jaya**, are often tinted with chemical dyes nowadays; the "duller", clay-coloured tones indicate natural dye. Stone axes partly encased in weaving may be offered to you, along with spears and bows and arrows. The shell breastplates worn by the "gentle warriors" of the Baliem Valley could make striking neckwear for women. Asmat carving finds its way to the market and is on sale in Asmat territory. The abstract beauty and strength of the finer objects will impress the connoisseur in you, but lesser works are now being produced for visitors, so study a little to be able to discriminate.

As a general lead, bargain to half price. However, Indonesians don't usually bring great conviction to the game. Note that valuable antiques should be checked and cleared for export—a good dealer will help.

Some like it hot. Indonesian cuisine is delicious, but watch out for those chilis!

EATING OUT

Rice is the staple food of most Indonesians; though in a few areas it's corn, sweet potatoes or sago. The word for cooked rice *(nasi)* is also applied to a whole meal. The usual accompaniments are coconut milk and spices, together with soy beans, peanuts and salted fish, which keeps better than fresh in the climate. Nevertheless there's plenty of seafood and fish even inland where rice farmers rear them in flooded paddy fields or big open pools, and chicken, goat, beef and buffalo. Pork is served only in Chinese restaurants in Islamic areas.

Indonesia's "coat of arms" is *nasi goreng*, fried rice with an egg on top, and it can turn up at any meal, including breakfast. *Babur kancang* (bean porridge) is another breakfast standby. *Nasi rames* is white rice with meat and vegetable side dishes; *mie goreng* replaces the rice with noodles. *Gado-gado,* an excellent luncheon dish, is a slightly cooked vegetable salad served with a spicy peanut sauce, while *pecal*, a more exotic version, combines soya bean cake, papaya and tapioca leaves. *Cap cai* is Indonesia's interpretation of chop suey. *Sop* is soup; *soto,* a thick soup, is made with the addition of coconut milk. Instead of bread you'll be served *krupuk*, large prawn crackers. *Sate,* rivalling *nasi goreng* as the national dish, is charcoal-cooked meat in tiny pieces on miniature bamboo skewers. Give it a squeeze of lime and dip it in peanut sauce.

Go easy on the *sambal,* a chili, lime and prawn paste. If you do catch fire, plain rice, cucumber or banana will help, while water or beer will make it worse. When the dish itself is too spicy for your taste, a squeeze of lime or lemon and a sprinkle of salt will help tone it down.

The Dutch invented the *rijsttafel* (rice table), a whole banquet of side dishes accompanying rice, and versions of it still presented in hotels are a good introduction to Indonesian eating pleasures, whatever purists say.

Jakarta can provide most things in the culinary line but each region has its specialities. In Yogyakarta the fried chicken *(ayam goreng)* is notably good but even better is a regional version called *mbok benek*, where the pieces are marinated in coconut milk beforehand. East Java has a good local fish called *badeng* and *rujak tjengor,* a curiosity-provoker which turns out to be cow's nose and bean curd. The Balinese have no inhibitions about pork and serve *babi guling* (roasted suckling pig) and *babi kecap* (pork in sweet soy sauce). The ducks you see quacking happily off to the rice fields don't suspect their coming glory as *bebek betutu* (duck broiled in banana leaves).

Prepare in advance to photograph such moments, rare in any lifetime.

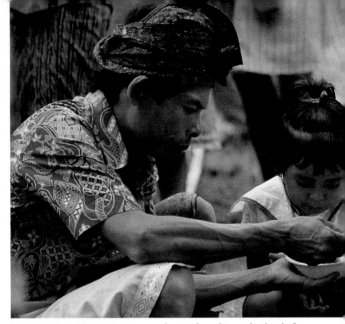

It's the people you'll remember. Serious, gentle, and eager to know more about you.

South Sulawesi has excellent fish all up the coast. *Pulu mara* is steamed fish in a spicy sauce, *ikan bakar* is baked fish. Quite a lot of buffalo meat is served; *soto makassar* is thick buffalo soup.

Padang (West Sumatra) has the spiciest cooking of all and some say the best. *Nasi padang* is lickety-hot rice. Hold off *rendang padang* (buffalo cooked in coconut milk) or, at least train on it conscientiously for a couple of days before ordering *deng deng,* with more chilis than meat, plus a sprinkling of chilis on top for good measure. In Sumatra *sate* is often served with rice cakes.

Among the many delicious desserts, try "sticky" rice steamed in banana stems and served with sugar-cane syrup. Steer off street ice cream. The fruit is out of this world. Peel open rambutans, mangosteens, snakefruit (*salak*) and gourmand-size passionfruit (*marquisa*). For thirst-quenchers, carry refreshing little *dukus.* You'll either love or detest *durian,* which Sumatrans claim is the

only fruit tigers eat. The taste has been compared to ripe camembert and old socks. There are all sorts of bananas, down to the sweet, finger-sized variety *(pisang mas)*.

In the beverage line, there's good beer (Bintang and Ankar) and a lemonade-beer shandy, Green Sands. Stronger alcoholic drinks are available in major hotels, and bottled alcohol can be bought in many supermarkets and the Sarinah department store, Jakarta. Muslim Indonesians don't touch it, so be prepared to order soft drinks or fruit juices for friends. Some native wines are brewed in a few places from rice and palm. There's a wide selection of fruit juices including *apokat* (avocados, tinned milk and flavouring), *es kelapa* (coconut water, coconut jelly and ice) and *marquisa*. The coffee and tea are good.

When dining with Indonesians, help yourself generously to rice, then take just a little from side dishes. Wait to be asked by your host to start eating or drinking. The left hand is considered unclean, so in situations where you're passing food or eating with your fingers, use the right hand. Don't empty your glass completely—it's polite to leave a token amount at the bottom.

BERLITZ-INFO

CONTENTS

A ACCOMMODATION

(See also CAMPING.) Major international hotels (5-star and down) are confined to the main cities or places of strong touristic interest; they offer all the usual amenities such as air-conditioning, room service and swimming pools. Sometimes, especially in high-country resorts, you'll find old Dutch hotels with all the charm of a vanished era.

A *wisma* or *pondok* is a guesthouse, comparable to a modest hotel in most parts of the world and often family-run. The staff is friendly and efficient; generally the rooms are clean, often with shower, flush toilet and air-conditioning. Some have restaurants attached and provide breakfast and room service. Note, though, that everything marked *wisma* isn't a hotel, the word can be applied to any kind of building.

A *losmen* is less expensive and you can choose whether or not to share a room (up to four beds). Toilet facilities are also shared. You can ask for meals to be sent in. A *penginapan* is even simpler and cheaper. Youth hostels and YMCAs are clean, offering basic accommodation, but a *losmen* can work out cheaper and is usually more fun.

In remote areas where there is no accommodation, it's considered normal practice to ask the local headman about families willing to put you up. You'll be offered a bed and meals, and should pay your hostess the price of the food. In any case, you should call on the headman in small communities to make your presence known.

All hotels add 21% tax and service charge to the bill.

Do you have any vacancies?	**Apakah masih ada kamar yang kosong?**
a single/double room	**kamar untuk satu orang/ kamar untuk dua orang**
with bath/shower	**dengan kamar mandi atau shower**

AIRPORTS

Sukarno-Hatta international airport in Jakarta is located 20 km (12 miles) from the city via an excellent toll highway. Formalities are rapid and courteous for in-coming travellers. A tourist information office, hotel booking centre and money changer with clearly displayed exchange rates are all indicated. If you depart from Sukarno-Hatta airport, allow plenty of time for getting there in case the inner city is piled into one of its notorious traffic jams. You'll find bookshops, restaurant, coffee-shop, bar, duty-free boutiques and gift shops in the well-planned, air-conditioned departure lounge. There's a departure tax unless you stay less than 24 hours, in which case you should report to the Garuda desk irrespective of the airline you're flying with. Reconfirm reservations, even on domestic flights, in advance. The domestic departure tax is sometimes included in the price of the ticket.

All Jakarta's legal taxis have meters, but you'll find non-official cars and mini-buses vying for custom. These are not metered and you have to agree on a price with the driver which may or may not include the highway toll.

Bali's *Ngurah Rai* international airport lies just south of Kuta Beach. There's a money changer and information counter. If you're not on a hotel pick-up service, pay for your taxi in advance at the indicated counter. There are gift shops, cafeteria and exchange desk in the departure lounge.

Medan's *Polonia* airport, about 2 km (1 mile) from the city, serves both domestic and international flights. Porters wear bright yellow. Taxis are available at the exit; outside the airport grounds you'll find *becaks* but they may not be able to take you right into the city.

Where's the bus for...?	**Manakah bus yang menuju ke...?**

BUSINESS HOURS B

Shopping complexes, supermarkets and department stores are open 9 a.m.–9 p.m. daily including Sunday. Government offices open 8 a.m.–3 p.m. Monday to Thursday inclusive, from 8 a.m.–11.30 a.m. Friday and 8 a.m.–2 p.m. Saturday. Business offices often have staggered hours. They may open 8 a.m.–4 p.m. or 9 a.m.–5 p.m. Some open a half-day Saturday. Banks open 8 or 8.30 a.m.–noon or 1 p.m. Hotel branches stay open longer, and money-changers are active all day.

CAMPING C

Most campers carry sheets of plastic to spread over a light pole frame. Allow a good overlap and tie the plastic down well to stop sagging during heavy rain. Plastic is also needed for a ground-sheet, and clothing and foodstuffs should be packed in plastic bags. Local people can be found to act as porters-cum-guides for a daily fee plus food. Do your research about the supplies you'll need, including torch, candles, mosquito net/coils/insect repellent. Don't forget snorkelling gear if applicable.

Is there a campsite nearby?	**Adakah tempat untuk berkemah disekitar sini?**
May we camp on your land?	**Bolehkah kami berkemah di tanah anda?**

CAR RENTAL

Short-stay visitors usually hire a taxi or chauffeur-driven car. Enquire at your hotel or at a Pacto or Nitour office, both reputable firms offering a multitude of travel services throughout Indonesia. If you travel long distances with a driver, he is responsible for car maintenance and fuel and will find his own accommodation. It's normal to pay for his midday meal and refreshments along the way, but he may choose to eat in a different place with other drivers and friends. You will almost certainly find him helpful in every way, so show your appreciation by tipping in proportion to his length of service.

Taxis can be hired by the hour or the day even for fairly long excursions. There are varying rates for out-of-town transport, and prices also differ according to the type and condition of the vehicles. (See also DRIVING, TAXIS.)

I'd like to hire a car for a day/a week.	**Saya ingin menyewa mobil untuk sehari/seminggu.**

CHILDREN

Take your children to Indonesia and the success of your trip is assured. Indonesian youngsters are brought up to be self-expressive and yet responsible to those smaller than themselves. They are well-behaved without being subjected to undue discipline. Children are considered precious. You can take yours to cultural events such as dance, gamelan, and puppet shows knowing that their enthusiasm won't give offence.

CLOTHING

Don't pack too much because you can supplement your wardrobe very cheaply here. Bring lightweight cottons including a long-sleeved blouse, shirt or T-shirt to protect your arms from the sun during prolonged sightseeing. Cotton underclothes are best; synthetic fibres are uncomfortable in the climate and can result in prickly heat. Boutiques on Bali offer a good range of beach clothes. Lengthy and repeated exposure to the sun can result in skin cancer, so wear a hat. Both men and women will find a sarong indispensable as a cover-up for visiting religious sites, as a wrap on the beach, even as an extra sheet in out-of-the-way places—small hotels often provide only one sheet and bedding is frequently damp. Some clever knotting and tucking and it will also convert into a sun-dress, a skirt in the evening or as beach shorts for men. Skimpy, revealing clothing is to be avoided except at beach resorts. Thongs are fine around the beaches, but closed, lightweight shoes are more practical for walking any distance.

Indonesians are fashion-conscious and so are many beach resort visitors, so prepare to dress up on occasion. Long-sleeved batik shirts are normal semi-formal evening wear for men. Discreet street clothing is expected for visiting government departments.

Some areas—such as Mt Bromo—can become downright cold, so you'll also need jeans and sweater or windproof jacket.

COMMUNICATIONS

Post offices are crowded and involve long, slow queues; it's much more convenient to use the services of large hotels which will take care of your mail even if you're not staying there. Make sure that all your important incoming and outgoing mail is registered.

Ask your correspondents to write your surname in capital letters, underlined, to avoid confusion. If you do go to the post office, take your own glue for stamp-sticking and ask to have mail franked before your eyes.

There's an express service for domestic mail. At post offices you can obtain blue envelopes marked *kilat* for airmail and yellow ones marked *kilat khusus* for express airmail. You'll need your glue here, too! Private delivery companies are reliable.

Hotels will also deal with faxes, telexes and telegrams. Indonesia has direct dialling for domestic and overseas calls.

airmail/registered	**pos udara/pos tercatat**
A stamp for this letter/ postcard, please.	**Saya perlu perangko untuk surat/kartupos ini.**

COURTESIES

Indonesians are instinctively gentle, courteous to an extreme, respectful to older people and conformist. They won't give you a straight answer if they don't know something or think they'll disappoint you. Pushing for it makes matters worse since they lose face in the process. When things seem slow, try not to show you're angry. An Indonesian who is *malu* (shamed) in front of others isn't likely to be helpful anyway.

Shake hands when you join and leave a gathering. The left hand is used in the toilet and is considered unclean. Use your right hand for passing things (food, cigarettes, gifts) and for eating. Don't start eating or drinking until invited to do so by the host (who's applying polite restraint himself) and leave a little at the bottom of the glass as a sign of appreciation. Pork and some shellfish are forbidden to Muslims, and beef to Hindus. In restaurants, do not return food to the kitchen even if it is cold; it would be considered extremely rude to do so.

Any decisive gesture (pointing, beckoning, placing hands on hips) is thought aggressive. Point with your thumb and attract attention with a wave. Don't indicate objects with your foot either (merchandise on the ground, for example). It's a sign of contempt. Crossing your legs so that the sole of your foot faces someone is impolite.

Don a sash to enter Hindu temples and keep off the walls so that you're not higher than the priest. As a general rule the most important person is supposed to stand tallest, which is why the Javanese often bob their heads when they cross in front of you. Don't touch people (including children) on the head, it's considered sacred. Remove your shoes before entering a mosque.

Small gifts (balloons, candy) will be appreciated by individual children who pose for pictures or help in other spontaneous ways. If you start handing out in a crowd you'll soon be surrounded; you'll need the patience of Job plus the strength of Hercules to cope.

"Hullo, Mister/Missus, where are you from?" is a stock greeting. A "hullo" back is all that's needed if you don't want to get involved. Don't be startled by cries of "Belanda!". The word used to mean Hollander but now is the term for any fair-skinned stranger.

CRIME

However little you're travelling with, you have more than most people here. Watch out for pickpockets. Carry cash in a belt or a bag with a strap that goes across or around the body, or better still, place valuables in the hotel strongbox. Don't wear jewellery likely to provoke envy. Don't place bags on the ground in public areas—they can vanish in a flash.

My ticket/wallet/passport has been stolen.	**Ticket saya/dompet saya/passpor saya telah dicuri orang**

CULTURAL CENTRES

These are good places to meet other nationals if you're staying any length of time. Most have libraries and can put you in touch with what's going on in the expatriate community.

Indonesian American Cultural Centre, Jl. Pramuka Kav. 30, Jakarta; tel. 881241, 8580536, 8582464.

The British Council, Wijaya Centre, Jl. Jend. Sudirman 71, Jakarta; tel. 587411. Also in Bandung.

Dutch Cultural Centre, Erasmushuis, Jl. Rasuna Said Kav. 53, Jakarta; tel. 512321.

Australian Cultural Centre, Fifth Floor, Citibank Building, Jl M.H. Thamrin 55, Jakarta; tel. 330824.

The American Women's Association (AWA), Agape House, Jl. Laser 12, Kebayoran Baru; tel. 771947, is an extremely active and well-informed group ready to share information about all aspects of life in Indonesia. Their handbook, *Introducing Indonesia*, provides invaluable advice for expatriates in the country.

CUSTOMS and ENTRY REGULATIONS

To enter Indonesia you will need a passport valid at least 6 months after the date of entry, and if you are travelling for business purposes you will also need a visa. A special permit, *Sulat Jalan,* is required for anyone wishing to visit Irian Jaya; it is issued by Dinas Intel Pam Pol MABAK in Jakarta or other regional police headquarters in Biak or Jayapura, and takes about two days.

If you're travelling with medication which may be mistaken for saleable drugs, bring a letter or prescription from your doctor. Weapons and ammunition are not allowed in. You may be asked about cameras, typewriters or electronic goods but problems are unlikely. Photographic and video equipment should be registered in your passport. Customs officers are courteous and reasonable. If you've nothing to declare, use the "Green Lane". (See also MONEY MATTERS.)

You are permitted to import duty-free: 150 cigars or 600 cigarettes or 300 g tobacco, less than 2 litres of alcoholic beverages in opened bottles, a reasonable quantity of perfume, and gifts up to a value of US$100.

When you leave home, ask at the Customs desk for the form setting out the allowances for your return.

I've nothing to declare.	**Saya tidak mempunyai apa-apa yang harus dilaporkan.**
It's for my personal use.	**Ini barang-barang untuk keperluan saya sendiri.**

CYCLES and MOTORCYCLES

There are plenty of bicycles for rent in Bali and Yogyakarta, and you don't need a licence to ride. In other areas where it's difficult to find suitable, well-maintained machines to hire, it may be worthwhile buying a second-hand model. Check all the safety features, especially tyre-treads, brake, bell and reflectors. Nearly every little settlement has a repair shop. Most roads in Java and Bali are sealed; some have cycle tracks. Bikes are a predominant means of transport in many places. For longer hauls, you can load both yourself and the machine on a bus. Traffic is hazardous, so bring or buy a helmet.

Carry an International Driving Permit if you intend riding a motorcycle. There are plenty for rent in Bali and Yogyakarta, with or without a driver. If there's a driver, you ride pillion, often a wise choice since a disproportionate number of foreigners is involved in traffic accidents on Bali. A helmet is essential.

Lock your bike securely when you leave it; if there's a bike park with attendant it's worth paying the small sum to have it looked after.

D DANGEROUS ANIMALS AND PLANTS

Out of more than 400 species of snake about five are poisonous. Avoid walking barefoot in vegetation, especially at night. If someone is bitten, apply a tourniquet, keep the person as still as possible and transport immediately to hospital. Since many plants, even ornamental shrubs in gardens, are toxic, don't pick leaves from unknown species and don't allow children to play with seeds or pods.

DRIVING

Roads vary from the good to the totally unbelievable. If you're heading off main routes, enquire about conditions beforehand. Most professional drivers are skilful but don't be afraid to speak out if you think yours is speeding. In cities, you'll be worried about the way he negotiates passing *becaks* and bicycles; on the open road you'll be appalled at the speed of buses, especially when they are overtaking. Avoid taking to the roads after nightfall when you'll be a danger yourself to pedestrians, animals and small vehicles with no lights.

Traffic (officially) drives on the left.

International Driving Permit	**Surat Ijin Mengemudi (SIM) Internasional**
Car registration papers	**Surat-surat kendaraan**
Where's the nearest service station?	**Dimanakah pompa bensin terdekat?**
Full tank, please.	**Fulteng/tolong diisi penuh.**
Check the oil/tyres/battery, please.	**Tolong periksa olinya/ban/aki.**
My car has broken down	**Mobil saya rusak.**

DRUGS

Holding, selling, importing and exporting narcotics is illegal and punishable by severe jail sentences and fines.

ELECTRIC CURRENT

Most hotels use 220 volts, 50 cycles and a round, two-pronged slim plug. Some provincial buildings are still on 110 volts. Bathroom shaver plugs usually have a transformer switch. Transformers for other appliances are available at larger hotels.

EMBASSIES

Australia	Jl. M.H. Thamrin 55, Jakarta; tel. 330824.
Canada	5th Floor, Wisma Metropolitan I, Jl. Jenderal Sudirman Kav. 29, PO Box, Jakarta; tel. 510709.
Great Britain	Jl. M.H. Thamrin 75, Jakarta; tel. 330904.
Netherlands	Jl. H.R. Rasuna Said Kav. S–3, Jakarta; tel. 511515.
New Zealand	Jl. Diponegoro 41, Jakarta; tel. 330552.
Singapore	Jl. H.R. Rasuna Said Kav. 2, Blok X/4, Jakarta; tel. 5201489.
USA	Jl. Merdeka Selatan 5, Jakarta; tel. 360360

GETTING TO INDONESIA

There are flights to Jakarta, Denpasar and Medan from all over the world and you'll see cheap tickets advertised in all national newspapers. Consult a reliable travel agent and get him to hunt around for the best deal. If you're travelling from continental Europe you'll probably find it cheaper to get your tickets in London, though discount fares are available in the Netherlands, Belgium, Germany, France, Austria, Italy and Switzerland. Canadians will probably find it advantageous to fly from the USA.

The sea route from Singapore to Sumatra is increasingly popular: there are five ferries daily to Tanjungpinang on the Riau archipelago, and from there boats sail via the Siak river to Pekanbaru in East Sumatra.

GIFTS

Business gifts and invitations are a universal formality, but tourists also need to plan ahead and bring little mementos from home. People will love to see photographs of your family, your house, business and home town. T-shirts with overseas place names are appreciated. In outlying districts children will flock around you, so stock up with candy, balloons and other lightweight items whenever you get the opportunity. In some areas, including Kalimantan and Irian Jaya, school pens and notebooks are much sought after. Many Indonesians smoke, so you may wish to offer adults cigarettes or tobacco (they probably prefer clove-scented cigarettes). If possible wrap gifts elegantly. An Indonesian will never open a gift in front of the giver.

Even apparently well placed officials are not well paid. A discreet sum of money could be the answer to bureaucratic problems.

GUIDES
If you're on an organized tour, guides will be provided wherever you go. Otherwise, hire one on the spot when you visit places of special interest such as *kraton* and temples. You can also hire a private guide for the length of your stay; your hotel reception or travel agency will be able to arrange it.

H HEALTH
(See also WATER.) Well before you leave home, consult your doctor about immunization for tetanus, polio, cholera and hepatitis. Have a dental check-up for good measure. Bring prescription medicines with you in sufficient quantity, and if you wear glasses, pack a spare pair in case of loss or breakage.

Your doctor or pharmacist will also advise on malaria tablets; remember to keep taking them for the required period of time after leaving Indonesia. Take every precaution against mosquitoes by using insect repellent, nets and coils.

Staff in reliable hotels and restaurants have usually been through an approved food-handling course. Nevertheless, the fact that salad ingredients need to be soaked for 20 minutes in a cleansing solution, then a further 20 minutes in purified water should alert you to the risk of raw vegetables. All fruit should be peeled.

Be wary of milk products, including ice cream unless you know the brand name is reputable. Street ice cream may contain unsterilized water. Avoid ice unless you know it's made on hygienic premises. What is normal for your hosts, who are probably immune, could be harmful for you. Meat and fish, particularly pork, seafood and shellfish, should be well-cooked.

Intestinal worms are common; some types enter through the sole of your feet, so always wear shoes. Bilharzia is a threat in some areas: don't swim in fresh water unless it's free-running.

Strict personal hygiene is essential—copy the Indonesians, who bathe at least twice a day and wash their hair frequently. Take a shower or bath when you come in from the street, and dry with talcum powder. Change into thongs indoors—they are sometimes provided by the hotel. In small or communal lodgings, wear rubber sandals in the bathroom and shower. In small hotels the bathroom may contain a waist-high tub of water for bathing *(mandi)*: stand on the floor, slosh yourself with water, soap yourself and rinse off. Don't get *in* the tub!

Cuts and abrasions should be promptly cleansed, treated and covered. Abrasions from coral and shells are particularly difficult to heal, so don't take risks in the water.

Wear a hat or buy yourself a parasol; protect your eyes with sunglasses and don't forget the sun-screen. Drink plenty of fluids, especially beneficial with a squeeze of lime, and keep your salt level up. Take a lesson from the Indonesians, who cover themselves from the sun, move slowly, are forever dousing themselves with water and often rest during the hottest part of the day.

A health kit is essential if you intend camping in nature reserves. Basic items are mosquito coils, antihistamine cream for insect bites, diarrhoea remedy, insect repellent, aspirin, gauze, antiseptic, sticking plaster.

Larger hotels have doctors and nurses on call. Pharmacies can supply most products and make up prescriptions, which hotel pharmacies are not qualified to do. Indonesians themselves prefer *dukun* (folk doctors) to western-style medicine—they are knowledgeable about herbal remedies, *jamu*, which are sold in commercial form in shops and markets.

HITCH-HIKING

This could be a fantastic experience, but the same precautions apply here as elsewhere. Women should not dress in a manner likely to be construed as provocative and should not travel alone. There's other cheap transport available, so why take the risk?

LANGUAGE   L

It's extremely easy to pick up key words in Bahasa Indonesia and string them together in comprehensible sentences. Everyone will respond when you try. Generally, the second to last syllable is stressed.

Vowels are pronounced:

a as in "r**a**ther"
e as in "m**e**t"
i usually as in "m**ee**t"; otherwise short as in "s**i**t"
o as in "**ou**ght"
u as in "t**wo**"
ai as in "l**i**ke"
au as in "c**ow**".

Consonants are generally pronounced as in English, with the following exceptions:

c as in "**ch**in"

g as in "**g**uest"

k as in English but almost silent at the end of a word

r well rolled, as in American English.

A word mispronounced may not be understood. Spelling was revised in 1972 but you may still see some old forms, especially for historical names which are sacred. Try to master at least the daily greetings and the words to say "thank you" and "goodbye". (See also USEFUL EXPRESSIONS.)

yes/no	**ya/tidak**
please/thank you	**tolong/terima-kasih**
Good morning/Good afternoon	**Selamat pagi/Selamat siang**
Good evening/Goodbye	**Selamat malam/Selamat tinggal**
Speak slowly, please	**Tolong berbicaranya perlahan-lahan.**

LAUNDRY and DRY-CLEANING

Most hotels offer a one-day service. Smaller places do an enthusiastic job hand-washing but colours are likely to fade and clothes may come back damp. Small towns don't have dry-cleaners, and very small towns don't have irons!

M MAPS

Hotel desks, travel agencies, local tourist offices and bookshops can supply maps of varying quality, depending on the number of outside visitors the area receives. Streets sometimes have "popular" names that aren't shown on the map even though they may always be used.

MEETING PEOPLE

You'll feel as though half Indonesia wants to know you from the moment you arrive. It can become tiring, so learn a few amusing or firm phrases in Bahasa to handle it, or else just smile and walk on. Many people want to practise their English. Indonesians usually shake hands on being introduced, both men and women. Physical contact (kissing, embracing) is not considered suitable public behaviour.

MONEY MATTERS

The national currency unit is the rupiah (rp). Banknotes come in denominations of 100, 500, 1,000, 5,000 and 10,000 rp. Coins, increasingly little used, are 5, 10, 50 and 100 rp.

There's no restriction on the importation of foreign money in cash or traveller's cheques, nor is there any problem in taking it out again—though it's always wise to keep exchange slips on you. You can export up to 50,000 rp in Indonesian currency. American dollars are convenient, but Deutschmarks, Swiss francs, Dutch florins, Australian and Singapore dollars and Japanese yen are exchangeable in touristic places or cities with expatriate workers. Money-changers give the best rates, followed by banks, then hotels.

You'll often have to bargain. You may not be used to it, but it's the custom here. Ask the price, offer about a third, then work your way up to a mutually agreeable sum. After so much effort on both sides, it would be insulting not to buy, so don't go too far with the game if you're not serious. Keep your finest skills for those who can afford it—there's no glory in winning a few rupiah off a *becak* man. (See also TIPPING.)

Could you give me some change?	**Dapatkah saya menukar uang?**
I want to change some pounds/dollars.	**Saya akan menukarkan beberapa uang dollar/poundsterling.**
Do you accept traveller's cheques?	**Apakah anda menerima pembayaran dengan traveller cheque?**
Can I pay with this credit card?	**Dapatkah saya membayar dengan kartu kredit ini?**

PHOTOGRAPHY

The country is irresistible photographically. Most people will allow you to photograph them; request permission first. Be discreet in temples and mosques, especially using flash. If you can, take a Polaroid along as well as your normal equipment so that you can give people a picture of themselves right away as a thank you. Restricted areas include ports. Museums sometimes ask a small fee (about 250 rp).

Silica gel packets kept with photographic equipment reduce problems of humidity. Don't leave your camera in direct sunlight or in a very hot place and don't leave film in it for more than a few days without taking a shot or two. Allow time for the lens to defog naturally when you leave an air-conditioned room.

Light is best in the early morning or late afternoon. At other times a filter will help, or try under-exposing by half a stop or more.

All normal makes of film including black and white and colour super-8 are available in the main cities, but you can't be sure you'll find them elsewhere. Check the date when you buy. If you stock up for a trip, make sure your reserves are kept in a cool place. A room refrigerator is fine, provided you take the film out a couple of hours before using it. Remember extra flash and camera batteries for longer trips.

Local processing is not ideal. Choose, if you can, to wait and have it done elsewhere. Customs officials are cooperative about not X-raying film provided you carry it in a separate bag for inspection.

May I take a picture?	**Bolehkah saya memotret?**

POLICE

Regular police wear a khaki cap, shirt and trousers and have their name and number on a badge. Traffic police have a white or green cap, a khaki or white and green uniform and display their name and number. Tourist police are being incorporated into some areas to help visitors (Yogyakarta). Under normal circumstances you'll find the service polite and affable. In police offices the bureaucratic system works very slowly.

PRESS, RADIO, TV

Notable among English-language dailies are the *Indonesian Observer, Jakarta Post, Indonesian Post* and *Surabaya Post*. They all contain news about current and forthcoming events as well as travel features of special interest to visitors. There's an ample selection of overseas publications, including the *International Herald Tribune* and *Straits Times* (from Singapore), *Time* and *Newsweek*. Copies of well-known overseas fashion and interior design periodicals are available; likewise the *Asian Wall Street Journal*. Tourist areas publish papers with information about their areas, available free in hotel foyers and tourist offices.

Hotels of any size offer satellite TV, so you can switch on to American news programmes and films; many have a video library.

Radio Republik Indonesia broadcasts programmes in English night and morning.

Have you any newspapers in English?	**Apakah anda mempunyai koran dalam bahasa Inggris?**

PRICES

To give you an idea of what to expect, here are some average prices in US dollars.

Airport transfer. Jakarta Sukarno-Hatta airport to all parts of Jakarta US$2 per person.

Car hire. US$60–100 per day (8 hrs), without driver. Driver fee US$10–15 per day.

Cigarettes. Indonesian: US$4–6 per box (10 packs); European/American: US$7–10 per box (10 packs).

Guide. English-speaking guide, half day: US$35, full day: US$50. For other languages the fee is more expensive.

Hotels (double room with bath). Western style: ★★★★★◊ US$200, ★★★★★ US$180, ★★★★US$150 per room per day. Breakfast: US$5–10, lunch US$8–20, dinner US$15–25, plus 15.5% service charge and tax. Guesthouse: room US$7.50–25 per day; breakfast US$1, lunch US$2, dinner US$2.

Meals. In a moderate restaurant, a Western-style meal, e.g. steak, US$10–15; Indonesian meal US$7–10. Self-service US$3–5.

Night clubs. Cover charge US$5–10. Hostess service US$5–10 per hour. An evening's entertainment, including dinner US$10–50.

Taxi fares. US$0.50 for the first km, US$0.25 each additional km.

Transport. *City bus,* non air-conditioned: US$0.15–0.25; air-conditioned US$0.70. *Intercity bus,* e.g. Jakarta–Bandung (3^1/2 hrs) US$2.50 non air-conditioned, US$4 air-conditioned. *Train* Jakarta–Yogyakarta (10 hrs), first class US$18; economy US$4. Children 6–12 pay 60%.

RELIGION R

Freedom of worship is written into the Constitution, and Indonesians will probably ask what you believe in. They respect everything except atheism which they equate with Communism, which arouses unhappy memories. Ninety per cent of the people are Muslim with a complicated background of Hinduism and animism. Bali is almost entirely Hindu. You will also meet Buddhists, Taoists and Christians, all with appropriate places of worship. There is no active synagogue.

The Islamic fast month, Ramadan, forbids eating, drinking and smoking from sunrise to sunset and varies in strictness according to region. It's followed by Lebaran, a time of rejoicing, visiting and exchanging gifts.

You'll be welcome at holy sites provided you're dressed appropriately and are not a distraction during prayers or ceremonies. Menstruating women aren't supposed to go into Hindu temples.

169

RESTAURANTS

In cities of any size you'll find international, Chinese, Japanese and Indonesian cuisine, but once you leave areas where there are numbers of Europeans the choice is limited, mainly to local and Chinese cooking. However, "limited" is hardly the word, for tremendous imagination and subtlety goes into the preparation of foodstuffs.

Hygiene is no worry in hotels and larger restaurants. Fruit, salad vegetables and ice are prepared under careful supervision. Even in small eating places Indonesians are conscious of the problem, especially for visitors, and will naturally offer you boiled and filtered water or tea as a beverage. *Warung* (food stalls) often have delicious cheap offerings but keep clear at first, until your system gets used to the change, especially in Jakarta. The *rumah makan* (eating house) is a midway stop between the *warung* and the *restoran* and its food is often superior.

To help you order...

I'd like...	**Saya ingin...**		*pepper*	**merica**
beer	**bir**		*potatoes*	**kentang**
bread	**roti**		*rice*	**nasi**
coffee	**kopi**		*salt*	**garam**
fish	**ikan**		*sandwich*	**roti sandwich**
fruit	**buah-buahan**		*soup*	**sop**
ice cream	**es krim**		*sugar*	**gula**
meat	**daging**		*tea*	**teh**
milk	**susu**		*water (iced)*	**air es**
orange juice	**air jeruk**		*wine*	**anggur**

...and read the menu

acar	*pickle salad*		hati	*liver*
ayam	*chicken*		ikan	*fish*
babi	*pork*		jambu biji	*guava*
bakmie	*noodles*		jeruk bali	*grapefruit*
bakpao	*large dumpling*		jeruk nipis	*lime*
belimbing	*star fruit*		kambing	*goat*
bihun	*noodles*		kecap	*soy sauce*
bistik	*steak*		keju	*cheese*
blewah	*melon*		kelapa	*coconut*
bubur	*porridge*		mangga	*mango*
delima	*pomegranate*		manggis	*mangosteen*
domba	*lamb*		markisa	*passion fruit*
gado-gado	*beans, veg .and*		martabak	*stuffed pancake*
	peanut sauce		mie	*noodles*

170

nanas	*pineapple*	sawo	*sapodilla plum*
nangka	*jackfruit*	sayur	*vegetables*
nasi	*rice*	semangka	*water melon*
otak	*brains*	soto	*soup*
pangsit	*small dumpling*	srikaya	*custard apple*
pisang	*banana*	telur	*egg*
salak	*snakeskin fruit*	udang	*prawns*

SMOKING S

Deli tobacco leaf, grown in North Sumatra, is reputed worldwide. Local cigarettes come crackly and clove-flavoured (*kretek*) or straight. Western brands are available throughout and relatively inexpensive. Many varieties of plug tobacco are sold in local markets.

TAXIS T

Only Jakarta and Surabaya have metered taxis. These can also be hired by the hour, the half-day and the day. If a driver says the meter is broken, either look for another cab or bargain on an hourly basis. Private taxis are unmetered and you should negotiate. You'll find taxis at hotel ranks where the staff will help you, or you can hail them in the street. Blue Bird is considered the best company. Don't be too ready to think your driver is deliberately taking you a long way round—Jakarta has a number of one-way streets which can turn a short distance into a marathon. Round the fare up to thank the driver for good service; for a short trip add about 100 rp.

THINGS TO BRING

You're bound to need most of these items if you're travelling far: alarm watch or clock, torch (flashlight), gifts, medicine kit, soap, sunglasses, sunscreen, tampons (unavailable in many areas outside Jakarta and Bali), toilet paper. Bring plenty of passport photos of yourself as you'll need them for various administrative reasons. If you're camping, you'll also need candles, mosquito net and insect repellent.

In the cities you should have no trouble finding your favourite brand of toothpaste, shampoo, conditioner and soap; well-known cosmetics and perfumes are also on sale. Don't buy these from street hawkers—it will probably turn out to be a poor, watered-down imitation of the real thing. (See also HEALTH.)

TIME

There are two attitudes to time in Indonesia—fairly punctual for businesses and important events and extremely flexible for everything else. The second type, frustrating to the average Westerner, is aptly described locally as *jam karet* ("rubber time").

The country has three official time zones: West Indonesia Standard Time, GMT +7, applies to Sumatra, Java, Madura and Bali; Central Indonesian Standard Time, GMT+8, is valid in Kalimantan, Sulawesi and Nusa Tenggara; East Indonesia Standard Time is GMT+9 for Maluku and Irian Jaya.

What time is it?	**Jam berapa sekarang?**

TOILETS

The further from main cities and big hotels you go, the more questionable the facilities. Ask for the WC (pronounced "way say") or *kamar kecil*. In smaller places, carry your own toilet paper. Where there are no flush toilets, use the plastic dipper and water from a tub you'll see alongside to flush them. To wash your hands when there's no basin and running water, use the dipper to pour water over them and let it splash on the floor, not back in the tub.

Where are the toilets?	**Dimanakah kamar kecil?**

TOURIST OFFICES

The Directorate General of Tourism (DGT) is located in Jakarta and administratively is under the Department of Tourism, Post and Telecommunications which has offices in all the main tourist destination areas. The Offices are known as KANWIL DEPPARPOSTEL or Regional Office of Tourism, Post and Telecommunications. Each of the 27 provinces of Indonesia also has its own tourist office which can be identified by the abbreviation DIPARDA (provincial tourist service) or BAPPARDA (provincial tourist agency). All these offices can offer assistance and information about their areas.

Tourist offices in Indonesia:

Bali: Kanwil Depparpostel X Bali & NTB, Bali & Nusa Tenggara Barat, Komplek Niti Mandala, Jl. Raya Puputan Renon, Denpasar 802355; tel. (0361)25649.

Central Java: Kanwil Depparpostel Vll Jawa Tengah, Jl. K.H.A. Dahlan No 2, Semarang 50241; tel. (024)311169.

Irian Jaya: Kanwil Depparpostel XVII Irian Jaya, Jl. Raya Abepura 17, PO. Box. 481, Jayapura 99112; tel. (0967)22446.

Jakarta: Kanwil Depparpostel V DKI Jakarta, Jl. K.H. Abdurrohim/Jl. Gatot Subroto, Jakarta 12710; tel. (021)511742.

Lampung: Kanwil Depparpostel IV Lampung & Bengkulu, c/o Kantor Telegraph, Jl. A. Yani, Kampung Cina, Benggkulu 38111; tel. (0721)55208.

South Sulawesi: Kanwil Depparpostel XIV Sulawesi Selatan. Jl. Pangeran Andi Petta Rani, Ujung Pandang 90222; tel. (0421)21142.

West Java: Kanwil Depparpostel VI Jawa Barat. Jl. K.H. Hasan Mustafa, Bandung 40263; tel. (022)72355.

West Nusa Tenggara: Diparda Nusa Tenggara Barat, Jl. Langko 70, Mataram, Lombok 83114; tel. (0364)217030.

West Sumatra: Kanwil Depparpostel II Sumatera Barat, Jl. Khatib Sulaeman, Padang Baru, Padang 25137; tel. (0751)28711.

Yogyakarta: Kanwil Depparpostel VII Yogyakarta, Jl. Adisucipto Km.7-8. P.O. Box 003, Yogyakarta; tel. (0274)5150.

TRANSPORT

Air. Garuda Indonesia is the national flag carrier, complemented by Merpati Nusantara, Bouraq and Mandala Airlines. Services are available to all provincial and district capitals and even remote areas. Smaller companies run charter flights: consult a good travel agent. In some places oil companies and missionaries will help, depending on space available. If you know your itinerary in advance, ask about inter-island fares in your home country, as an international flight on Garuda may qualify you for domestic discount. If you buy tickets in Indonesia, shop around and compare fares, since they differ considerably. Baggage allowance is normally 20 kg; it may be less on lighter aircraft but excess is often disregarded. Domestic airport delays are fairly common, often as a result of poor weather conditions.

Domestic head offices in Jakarta:
Garuda, Jl. Merdeka Selatan 13; tel. 3801901
Merpati, Jl. Patrice Lumumba 2; tel. 413608, 417404
Bouraq, Jl. Patrice Lumumba 1–3; tel. 6595326
Mandala, Jl. Garuda 76; tel. 413480

Trains. There are rail services for Java and part of Sumatra. The main routes are Jakarta–Yogya–Solo–Surabaya and Jakarta–Semarang–Surabaya, and the two link up. The *Bima* night express (via Yogya) is air-conditioned and has sleeping accommodation, two people to a compartment in first class, three in economy class. The *Mutiara* (via

Semarang) has air-conditioning and reclining seats. The *Parahiyangan* (Jakarta–Bandung) leaves several times a day, air-conditioning on some services, electric fans on others. Booking is disorganized, but once you're on board the experience is pleasant. To avoid the hassle of booking yourself, use an agent. Surabaya and Jakarta have several rail stations, so make sure you understand the departure details.

Long-distance buses. They are inexpensive but uncomfortable and frankly dangerous. The same applies to Colt minibuses. Drivers seem to lose all sense of survival once they get behind the wheel.

Ferries and boats. Depending on the region's stage of development, water transport may range from vehicular and passenger ferries (from Surabaya to Madura, for example), to simple bamboo rafts which are poled across streams. Sailboats, outriggers or motorized vessels can be hired for short cruises at most beach fronts. For information about regular services, consult the state-owned shipping company PELNI or a travel agent. If you want to try your luck on a Buginese *pinisi*, enquire at the port of departure that interests you.

City buses. They are cheap, crowded and difficult for foreigners as there aren't any route maps.

Becaks. This picturesque form of transport, a highly-coloured pedicab, literally folk-art on wheels, is being phased out. *Becak* men work hard, earn next to nothing and are prone to debilitating diseases due to their gruelling trade. Nevertheless, when they finally disappear from the streets they will face an even grimmer life unemployed. They inevitably overstate their price with foreigners but are quick to settle on a fair one. Agree about it before you start off, but don't be mean.

Helicaks and bajais. Two-passenger vehicles powered by a motor-cycle engine which will give you all the thrills of a fairground as you tear almost totally unprotected through city traffic. Settle the price beforehand (you'll be speechless later anyway). They are quick and convenient and sooner or later you'll find yourself in one.

Opelets and bemos. The name varies but basically these are minivans following either a fixed route or operating in a specified van zone. They also go long-distance between towns. Enquire at the local Colt station.

W WATER

Tap water is not fit for drinking and needs to be boiled for 20 minutes and stored in sterilized containers. The carafe water in your hotel is safe; otherwise, keep to bottled drinks and, if you're super-cautious, use a straw instead drinking from a glass. Use bottled or carafe water for cleaning your teeth. However, logic will tell you there's a limit to every precaution and your eating utensils were almost certainly washed in non-treated water.

Is this drinking water?	**Apakah air ini boleh diminum?**
a bottle of mineral water	**satu botol air putih**

WEIGHTS AND MEASURES
Indonesia uses the metric system.

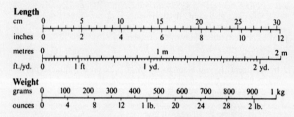

Length

Weight

USEFUL EXPRESSIONS U

Excuse me/You're welcome	**permisi/terimi-kasih kembali**
where/when/how	**dimana/kapan/bagaimana**
how much	**berapa**
yesterday/today/tomorrow	**kemarin/hari ini/besok**
day/week/month/year	**hari/pekan/bulan/tahun**
left/right	**kiri/kanan**
up/down	**naik/turun**
good/bad	**bagus/tidak bagus**
big/small	**besar/kecil**
cheap/expensive	**murah/mahal**
hot/cold	**panas/dingin**
old/new	**tua/baru**
open/closed	**buka/tutp**
here/there	**disini/disana**
free/occupied	**kosong/terpakai**
easy/difficult	**mudah/susah**
Does anyone here speak English?	**Adakah disini seseorang yang dapat berbicara dengan basasa Inggris?**

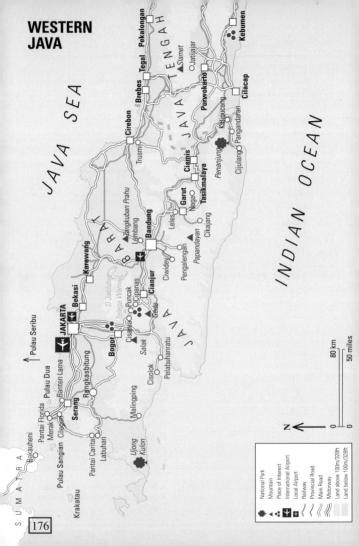

EASTERN JAVA

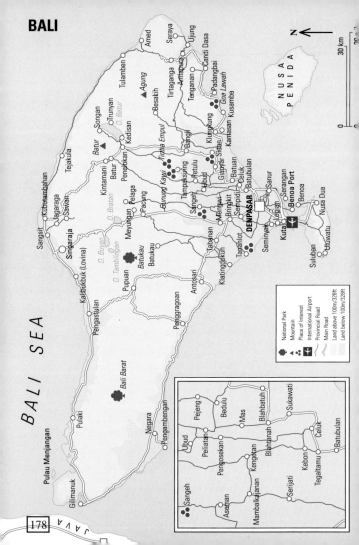

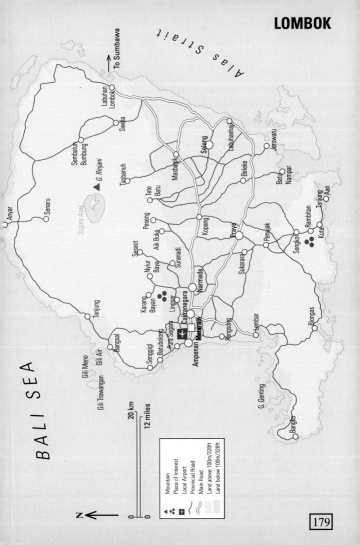

LOMBOK

Alas Strait

To Sumbawa

Labuhan Lombok

Swela

Sembalun Bumbung

▲ *G. Rinjani*

Segara Anak

Anyar

Senaru

Sapit

Selong

Masbagik

Labuhanhaji

Jerowaru

Timbanuh

Tete Batu

Beleke

Batu Nampar

Tanjung Aan

Peseng

Kopang

Praya

Rambitan

Kuta

Sesaot

Alik Buka

Penujak

Sengkol

Nyiur Baya

Suranadi

Sukarara

Karang Bayan

Lingsar

Narmada

Cakranegara

Mataram

Tanjung

Bangsal

Senggigi

Batubolong

Pura Segara

Ampenan

Pengsong

Rembar

Blongas

Gili Meno

Gili Air

Gili Trawangan

G. Genting

Bangko

BALI SEA

20 km

12 miles

N

Mountain
Place of Interest
Local Airport
Provincial Road
Main Road
Land above 100m/328ft
Land below 100m/328ft

SUMATRA

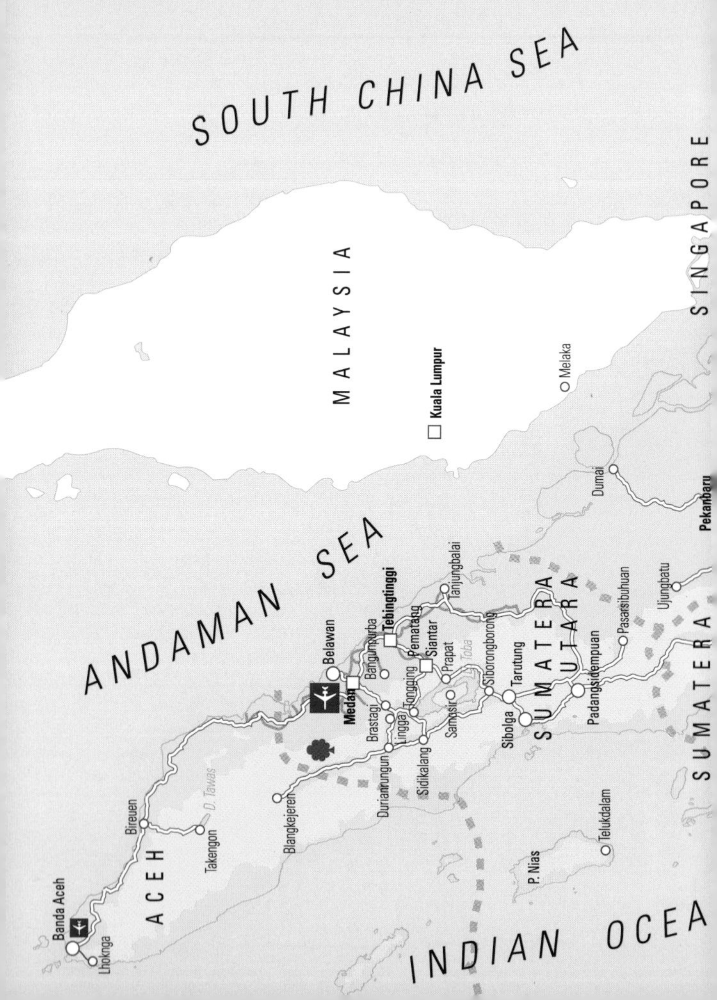

SOUTH CHINA SEA

SINGAPORE

MALAYSIA

□ Kuala Lumpur

○ Melaka

ANDAMAN SEA

Dumai

Pekanbaru

Tanjungbalai

Belawan

Tebingtinggi

Pematang

Bangunpurba

Medan

Siantar

Kisaran

Prapat

Brastagi

Lingga

Samosir

Siborongborong

Pasarsibuhuan

Ujungbatu

○ Sidikalang

Duriantungun

Tarutung

S U M A T E R A

U T A R A

Sibolga

Padangsidempuan

S U M A T E R A

Takengon

D. Tawar

Blangkejeren

Bireuen

P. Nias

Telukdalam

A C E H

Banda Aceh

Lhokruga

INDIAN OCEA

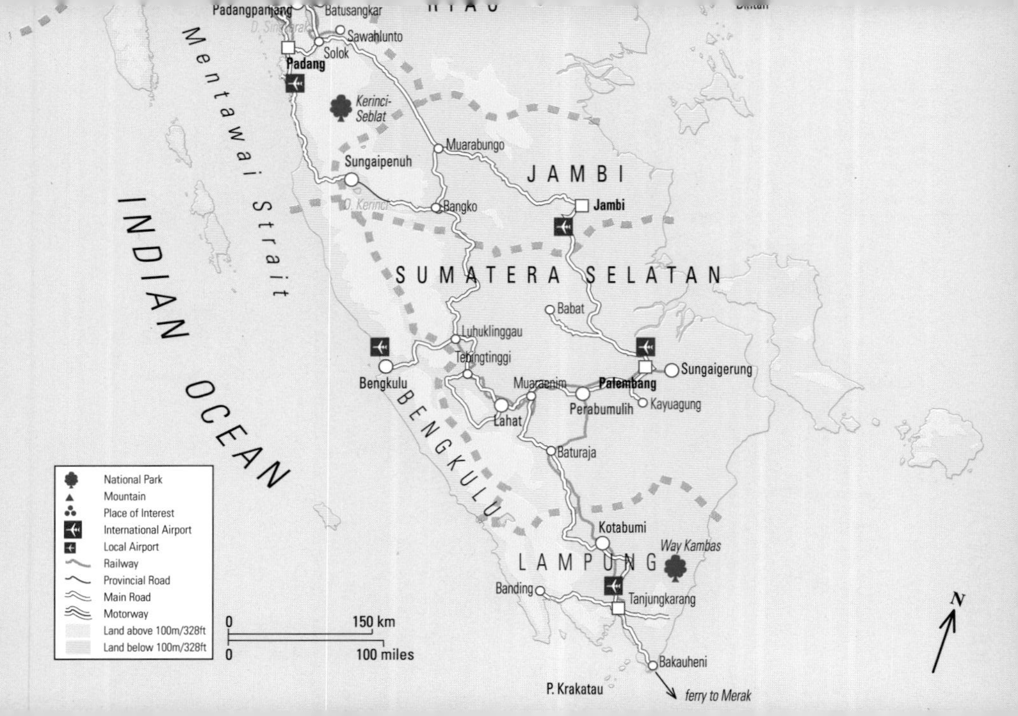

N

RIAU

JAMBI

SUMATERA SELATAN

BENGKULU

LAMPUNG

Sungaigerung

Kayuagung

Palembang

Perabumulih

Babat

Baturaja

Muaraenim

Lahat

Kotabumi

Way Kambas

Tanjungkarang

Bakauheni

Ferry to Merak

Banding

P. Krakatau

Jambi

Muarabungo

Bangko

Sungaipenuh

Kerinci-Seblat

to Kerinci

Luhukinggau

Tanjngtinggi

Muarabeliti

Bengkulu

Padang

Solok

Sawahlunto

Batusangkar

Padangpanjang

Mentawai Strait

INDIAN OCEAN

150 km

100 miles

0

National Park
Mountain
Place of Interest
International Airport
Local Airport
Railway
Provincial Road
Main Road
Motorway
Land above 100m/328ft
Land below 100m/328ft

KALIMANTAN

CELEBES SEA

SULAWESI

S U L A W E S I
U T A R A

Manado Bitung
Airmadidi Kema
Tondano

Tolitoli

Belang

Gorontalo
Suwawa
Imandi Kotamobagu

Sonjol

Donggala

Tanjung Api
Luwuk

Palu
Lore Lindu
Poso
Gimpu
Watutau
Katoposa

S U L A W E S I
T E N G A H

Morowali

S U L A W E S I
S E L A T A N

Saroako

B A N D A   S E A

andadiwata
Rantepao
Tana Toraja
Palopo

Majene
Makale
Rantemario

S U L A W E S I
T E N G G A R A

Pinrang
Rapang
Pare Pare
Singkang

Kolaka
Kendari

Bone

N

Maros
Bantimurung
Ujung Pandang

0   200 km
0   120 miles

Sungguminasa Bulukumba

Baubau

🌳 National Park
▲ Mountain
○ Place of Interest
✈ Local Airport
━ Main Road
    Land above 100m/328ft
    Land below 100m/328ft

F L O R E S   S E A

183

IRIAN JAYA

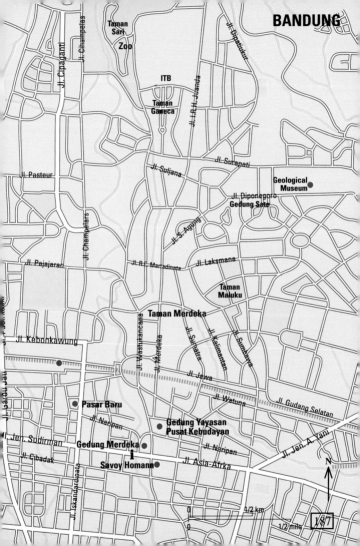

YOGYAKARTA

0   1/2 km

0   1/2 mile

N

Winongo

Butung

Jl. Kyai Mojo

Jl. Sindunegaran

Jl. Magelang

AM. Sangaji

Jl. I. C. Simanjuntak

Jl. Cik ditiro

Jl. Diponegoro   Jl. Jend Sudirman   Jl. Solo

Affandi

- Monumen Diponegoro

Jl. Mangkubumi

Jl. Atmo Sukarto

Jl. H.O.S. Cokroaminoto

Jl. Pringgo Kusuman

Jl. Keri- tiranlor

Jl. Let. Jend. Suprapto

Winongo

Jl. P. Mangkubumi

i

Jl. Suprapto

Jl. Dr. Sutomo

Pakualamen •

Jl. Wahidin

Balai Peneli Batik Kesayi •

• Pasar

Jl. Sultan Agung

Jl. Kusumaneg

Jl. K. H. Ahmad Dahlan

• Paket Post

Jl. Wakhmansyim

Museum Sonobudoyo •

Alun-alun Lor

Jl. Brig. Jend. Katamso

Jl. Hafid 66

Jl. Taman Siswa

Jl. Battah

Kraton •

Code

Taman Sari •

Alun-alun Kidul

Jl. May. Jen. Sutoyo

Jl. Parangtritis

Jl. Kol. Sugiyono

Jl. Menteri Supeno

Perjoangan Museum •

DENPASAR

Abiankapas

Jl. Nusa Indah

Jl. Kecubung

Jl. Satru

Jl. S. Parman

Jl. Nti Mandala

1/2 mile

1/2 km

N

Jl. Pica

Jl. Melati

St. Joseph's
Catholic Church

Jl. Kepundung

Jl. Pattimura

Pura Jagatnata
Museum Bali

Catur Muka

Kelandis

Jl. Putra

University
Udayana

Jl. Veteran

Jl. Hasanudin

Jl. Pangilma Besar
Sudirman

Jl. Raya Puputan

Alun-alun Puputan

Gajah Mada

Jl. Kartni

Jl. Jend A. Ya

Pasar Badung

Jl. Diponegoro

Jl. Badung

Jl. Nakula

Pasar Kumbasari

Jl. Thamrin

Pemecutan
Palace

Jl. Buru

Jl. Seabudi

Jl. Badung

Jl. Imam Bonjol

Jl. Teuku Umar

189

INDEX

An asterisk (*) next to a page number indicates a map reference. Where there is more than one set of page references, the one in bold type refers to the main entry. For index to Practical Information, see pp. 154–155.

INDEX